D1608071

SERMON IN A SENTENCE

St. Thomas Aquinas

SAINT
THOMAS
AQUINAS

SERMON IN A SENTENCE

*A Treasury of Quotations
on the Spiritual Life*

FROM THE WRITINGS OF

St. Thomas Aquinas

DOCTOR OF THE CHURCH

*Arranged according to the Virtues of
the Holy Rosary
and Other Spiritual Topics*

Selected and Arranged by
JOHN P. McCLERNON

IGNATIUS PRESS   SAN FRANCISCO

Cover art by Christopher J. Pelicano
Cover design by Roxanne Mei Lum

Frontispiece by John Herreid

© 2007 Ignatius Press, San Francisco
ISBN 978-1-58617-185-8
Library of Congress Control Number 2006939363
Printed in the United States of America ∞

The more a soul has been modeled on its Creator in this world, the more it will be like Him in the life to come; and the more it will be like Him, the greater will be its bliss, the more it will give glory to God, and the more it will be useful to every creature.

—St. Thomas Aquinas

DEDICATION

This work is dedicated to my wonderful and support-
ive wife, Mary, and to the fruit of our marriage, the
five beautiful children with whom God has blessed us:
Christopher, Clare, Catherine, David, and Stephen.

My good friend and fellow Third Order Dominican
Lorne Thomas is to be thanked for his ever-present support and advice. Lorne's knowledge and appreciation of
the writings and teaching of St. Thomas Aquinas has
proven invaluable to me. He is without doubt a tried
and true ambassador for the Angelic Doctor.

Special thanks goes out once again to my mother, Judy
McClernon, whose advice and assistance in sorting
through and selecting these "spiritual gems" from St.
Thomas have been so helpful.

Last, but certainly not least, I wish to thank St. Thomas
Aquinas for the monumental written legacy he has left
to the Catholic Church and, for that matter, the world.
They are certainly timeless, to be treasured by scholars,
theologians, religious, and lay people for all times and
places. The Angelic Doctor was just that: a miraculous
gift of God to a humanity that even seven hundred years
after him still hungers for the Eternal Light of Truth, as
given us in Jesus Christ, His Son. St. Thomas is the real
author of this book. It is an honor to be used as an instru-
ment in bringing his advice and teachings to souls seeking a tried and true path to holiness and sanctity.

CONTENTS

FOREWORD

At one point in his studies, Thomas Aquinas was called by some of his fellow students a "dumb ox". They were not aware of the depths of his concentration or of the thoroughness he employed while pursuing his objects of investigation. What appeared sometimes to be slowness of response was, in reality, his being "lost in thought". It was his teacher, St. Albert the Great, who set the students straight by predicting: "One day, his bellowing will be heard around the earth."

This prediction is fulfilled in Thomas' theology being taught in seminaries around the world and in his Eucharistic hymns and *Corpus Christi* liturgy resounding down the centuries in Catholic churches everywhere.

It is characteristic of Thomas' pursuit of truth that it be as exhaustive as possible. His synthesis of Aristotle's philosophy with his own Christian faith is an example. "Truth, from whatever source!" was his operating axiom. He would start with the best that human reason provided and "top off" the subject with appropriate revelation. The full truth, in the Dominican tradition, was his objective.

In his life, St. Thomas practiced what he preached. In the midst of fame and honors, he was a humble man, knowing the truth and living it. Despite his gigantic efforts in searching for truth in the wisdom of others, he attributed most of his learning to God's help, imparted to him as he prayed before the crucifix. His simple life-style as a religious made it possible for him to spend most of his time in prayer and study and in sharing the fruits of his contemplation with others.

In our modern times we might well follow the example of this medieval saint. In our "now generation" we need to move beyond the external senses and into the realm of thought. Providing time and interest for "thinking about things" would be a good discipline, applicable to our everyday life. Prayerfully thinking about God and His creation could enrich that daily life and prepare us for the happiness of the life yet to come. The well-chosen words of St. Thomas as presented in this little book will be an excellent guide in our transition from this life into the next.

Father Edward Robinson, O.P.
Dominican Priory of St. Albert the Great
Irving, Texas

INTRODUCTION

There are many Catholics who would like nothing better than to read the actual writings of the Church's spiritual giants. But how many do? The culture of today leads us to embrace such busy lifestyles. All too often the time needed to feed the soul takes a back seat, and one ends up spiritually starved. The *Sermon in a Sentence* series is designed for just such a person.

Imagine spending a few minutes with St. Thomas Aquinas, a Doctor of the Church and considered by many scholars as her greatest theologian and philosopher. The depth of knowledge and spiritual wisdom granted this thirteenth-century Dominican friar continues to enlighten Christianity today as it has for the past seven hundred years. Although certainly one of the world's greatest minds, he lived as an unassuming, humble, and pious friar of the Order of Preachers. The "Angelic Doctor", as the Catholic Church affectionately calls him, beckons souls to embrace the pursuit of Eternal Truth, and to embark on sure paths leading to the source of life and all beauty: the Eternal Godhead. The gifted insights of the great Aquinas have led many a scholar, theologian, religious, and layman to a deeper walk with God, and a better understanding of the Catholic Faith. This book has been designed to bring the inspiration of his words to you in a very simple and direct format.

Hundreds of short quotations taken from the writings and sayings of St. Thomas have been classified by the

Christian virtues of which they speak and then arranged to complement the Rosary, proceeding from the first joyful mystery (the Annunciation, with its virtue of humility) to the fifth glorious mystery (the Crowning of Mary, with its virtue of devotion to Mary). The Luminous Mysteries, introduced by John Paul II as an optional addition to the Rosary, are also included. For those who choose to use these excerpts for meditation while reciting the Rosary, we have placed a type ornament after the tenth one, to mark the end of a decade. Additional quotations follow, for use with a Rosary or for separate meditation. A selection of quotations on other spiritual topics of interest follows, bringing the reader a sample of St. Thomas' insights into such subjects as prayer and the Church.

It is hoped that this little book will serve as an effective introduction to one of our world's greatest spiritual masters. May these quotes and short sayings find a place in your heart and soul and draw you closer to our Lord Jesus Christ, Whom St. Thomas Aquinas loved and served so well.

ACKNOWLEDGMENTS

The author gratefully acknowledges the following sources and the permissions granted to reprint excerpts:

Aquinas's Shorter Summa. St. Thomas Aquinas's Own Concise Version of His Summa Theologica. St. Thomas Aquinas. Reprint of *Light of Faith: The Compendium of Theology.* Manchester, N.H.: Sophia Institute Press, 2002. Originally published in English in 1947 as *The Compendium of Theology* by B. Herder Book Company. Copyright 1993, 2002 by Sophia Institute Press, Manchester, N.H.

Catena Aurea. Commentary on the Four Gospels. Collected Out of the Works of the Fathers. St. Thomas Aquinas, Vol. I, part I and II. Boonville, N.Y.: Preserving Christian Publications, Inc., 2000. First published in 1842 by John Henry Parker, London.

Summa Theologica. First Complete American Edition in Three Volumes. St. Thomas Aquinas. Translated by the Fathers of the English Dominican Province. Vols. two and three. New York, N.Y.: Benziger Brothers, Inc., 1947. Copyright 1947 by Benziger Brothers, Inc. Reprinted with the permission of The Glencoe/McGraw Hill Companies.

The Aquinas Catechism. A Simple Explanation of the Catholic Faith by the Church's Greatest Theologian. St. Thomas Aquinas. Manchester, N.H.: Sophia Institute Press, 2000. Previously published as two books: *The Three Greatest Prayers* (Manchester, N.H.: Sophia Institute Press, 1990) and *God's Greatest Gifts* (Manchester, N.H.: Sophia Institute Press, 1992). Copyright 2000 by Sophia Institute Press, Manchester, N.H.

The Aquinas Prayer Book. The Prayers and Hymns of St. Thomas Aquinas. Translated and edited by Robert Anderson and Johann Moser. Manchester, N.H.: Sophia Institute Press, 2000. Originally published in 1993 by Sophia Institute Press under the title *Devoutly I Adore Thee.* Copyright 1993, 2000 by Robert Anderson and Johann Moser.

The Homilies of St. Thomas Aquinas on the Epistles and Gospels for the Sundays of the Christian Year to which are Appended the Feast-Day Homilies. Translated by John M. Ashley, B.C.L. Fort Collins, Colo.: Roman Catholic Books, 1996. First published in 1873.

The Ways of God for Meditation and Prayer. Saint Thomas Aquinas. Manchester, N.H.: Sophia Institute Press, 1995. Originally published in 1946 by Basilian Press, London, Ontario. Translated by Raissa Maritain and Margaret Sumner, with minor corrections and revisions by Sophia Institute Press. Copyright 1995 by Sophia Institute Press, Manchester, N.H.

Thomas Aquinas: Selected Philosophical Writings. Selected and translated by Timothy McDermott. Oxford World's Classics. Oxford, England: Oxford University Press, 1998. Copyright 1993 by Timothy McDermott. By permission of Oxford University Press.

Thomas Aquinas: Selected Writings. Edited by Rev. M. C. D'Arcy. Fort Collins, Colo.: Roman Catholic Books, n.d. Originally published by E. P. Dutton and Co., 1950.

ABBREVIATIONS

C   *The Aquinas Catechism: A Simple Explanation of the Catholic Faith by the Church's Greatest Theologian*, by St. Thomas Aquinas. Manchester, N.H.: Sophia Institute Press, 2000.

CA   *Catena Aurea: Commentary on the Four Gospels Collected out of the Works of the Fathers*, by St. Thomas Aquinas. Vol. 1, parts 1 and 2, St. Matthew. Albany, N.Y.: Preserving Christian Publications, 2000.

H   *The Homilies of Saint Thomas Aquinas upon the Epistles and Gospels for the Sundays of the Christian Year, to Which Are Appended the Feast-Day Homilies*, by St. Thomas Aquinas. Translated by John M. Ashley, B.C.L. Fort Collins, Colo.: Roman Catholic Books, 1996. First published in 1873.

P   *The Aquinas Prayer Book: The Prayers and Hymns of St. Thomas Aquinas*. Translated and edited by Robert Anderson and Johann Moser. Manchester, N.H.: Sophia Institute Press, 2000.

SP   *Thomas Aquinas: Selected Philosophical Writings*. Selected and translated by Timothy McDermott. Oxford: Oxford University Press, 1993.

SS   *Aquinas's Shorter Summa: The Light of Faith: The Compendium of Theology*, by St. Thomas Aquinas. Manchester, N.H.: Sophia Institute Press, 1993.

ST   *Summa Theologica*, by St. Thomas Aquinas. Translated by the Fathers of the English Dominican Province. New York: Benziger Brothers, 1947.

T   *Thomas Aquinas: Selected Writings*. Edited by Rev. M. C. D'Arcy. Fort Collins, Colo.: Roman Catholic Books, n.d.

W   *The Ways of God for Meditation and Prayer*, by St. Thomas Aquinas. Manchester, N.H.: Sophia Institute Press, 1995.

St. Thomas Aquinas

(1225–1274)

Doctor of the Church

Friar, Priest, and Patron of Academics,
Catholic Universities, Colleges, and Schools

With the possible exception of St. Augustine, no one person has had such a far-reaching, permanent impact on Christian theology and philosophy as St. Thomas Aquinas, a humble thirteenth-century Dominican friar who put his whole life's work into understanding, teaching, preaching, and defending the truth of Christ and His Catholic Church. Known as a man of few words and a pronounced taste for solitude and reflection, his mind and heart were completely wrapped up in the higher things of God. These saintly characteristics were not immediately understood by some of his fellow Dominican seminarians and teachers, who initially referred to Thomas as "the dumb ox", mainly due to his noted silence and large, bulky figure. However, the sheer brilliance and vast intellectual capacities of this friar would eventually unfold. While at Cologne, Thomas studied under the famed St. Albert the Great, who, along with many of the students, soon noticed that Thomas was able to answer theological questions and problems clearer and better than he. This great Dominican master exclaimed, "We have called Thomas 'dumb ox', but I tell you his bellowing will be yet heard to the uttermost parts of the earth."

Thomas was born into the Aquino family in 1225 or 1226, a few years after the death of St. Dominic, the founder of the Dominican Order. The Aquinos were an aristocratic Italian family with an ancestry traced back to Lombard kings. The actual place and date of his birth are not known for sure, but it is assumed he was born at the family's main castle in Roccasecca, which lies between Rome and Naples. A few miles from Roccasecca stood the most famous of Italian monasteries, Monte Cassino, whose abbot was Thomas' uncle. At the age of nine the young Thomas was entrusted to the monks at the Benedictine school next to the cloister. This was a normal practice for upper-class families connected with monasteries. It is apparent that even from youth Thomas was chiefly interested in placing his mind and heart on the things of God. He was popular with school friends, but usually preferred solitude and silence. Many years later the aged monks recalled how studiously Thomas delved into their manuscripts, how he asked them questions indicative of great intelligence, and how pious the boy was at prayer.

When Thomas reached the age of fourteen he was sent to the University of Naples, where he was to begin a seven-year undergraduate education common to all European universities at that time. There his studies focused on logic (including Aristotle), Latin literature, advanced natural sciences, and philosophy. It was during these years in Naples that Thomas became more and more attracted to the youthful and vibrant Dominican Order (also known as the Order of Preachers), whose members lived a simple, austere, evangelical religious life, while also stressing intellectual formation and preaching. He regularly attended the Dominican church in Naples and became friendly with the friars there. Thomas desired to dedicate his life to God in this way, and at the age of nineteen he was received as a novice and clothed in the Dominican habit. News of this decision quickly made its way to Roccasecca, where the Aquino family was furious, not over his religious vocation, but rather that this son of a noble family had chosen the poor, socially scorned, mendicant Order of Preachers. His mother, Theodora, fully expected her son Thomas to be a great churchman somewhere else, perhaps as the abbot of the famed Benedictine monastery of Monte Cassino.

An Aquino family drama soon unfolded, with urgent and well-connected appeals made to the Archbishop of Naples and even to the Pope in order to deter Thomas' plans. At that time, Thomas was hurried off by the Dominicans to the Master General's convent in Rome, and from there on to Western Europe. This trip, however, was not to be completed. His mother arranged to have Thomas' travel party intercepted by two of his older brothers, who then forcibly brought him back to the family castle in San Giovanni, and then on to Roccasecca, where he was locked up in a large room. It is not known for sure how long Thomas was kept in this confinement, but it was most probably for one to two years. This was not idle time in any way for Thomas, whose sisters secretly passed along books for their brother to study. (These were provided by the Dominican friars in Naples.) It was during these years that he studied Aristotle's *Metaphysics* and the most popular theological book of the thirteenth century, Peter Lombard's famed *Sentences* (an extensive collection of the opinions of the early Church Fathers). While confined, Thomas also delved into an intense and thorough study of the Bible and learned by heart many long passages of Sacred Scripture.

On his deathbed years later Thomas revealed a now well-known account that occurred during this period of confinement. A few of his brothers attempted to dampen his religious vocation by sending into his room a beautiful but loose woman to tempt him. Thomas seized a burning log from the fire and drove her out and then drew a cross on the wall with the embers. He prayed fervently to God to grant him the gift of perpetual chastity, at which time two angels miraculously appeared and girded him tightly with a cord around his waist. Thomas was rewarded with one of the most chaste and pure hearts ever known to man; his confessor later claimed that he never suffered from carnal thoughts or temptations of the flesh.

The Aquino family finally began to yield, eventually recognizing Thomas' unwavering determination to serve God as a Dominican. They also received pointed reprimands from both the Pope and the Emperor. Finally a band of disguised Dominicans, with the help of his sisters, helped Thomas escape through a castle window and then joyfully took him to Naples. They found him well educated, as if he never left formal studies. Thomas' mother would later admit that a hermit visited her not long after she had conceived Thomas, while she was still unaware of her pregnancy. This hermit prophesied that her new son would be called Thomas, that he would be unrivaled in holiness and knowledge, and, in spite of the family's objections, that he would join the Dominican Order.

The Dominicans sent Thomas to Cologne in order to complete his studies under the most renowned teacher of his day who would later be declared a Doctor of the Church: St. Albert the Great. Initial references to the quiet-mannered, bulky Thomas as the "dumb ox" quickly dissipated, as his brilliance and intellectual capacities became apparent to all. Albert moved Thomas to a cell beside his own, frequently took long walks with him, and often invited the young friar to impart his knowledge and opinions. Thomas proved to be a model friar, excelling in humility, piety, and learning. It was at Cologne that Thomas lectured under this great Dominican master, supervised students' work, and corrected essays. He demonstrated a great talent for imparting knowledge, along with deep religious fervor. The Mass and the Eucharist would always be central to Thomas' spirituality and love of God, and during these years at Cologne Thomas received Holy Orders. One of his early biographers noted that "when Thomas consecrated at Mass, he would be overcome by such intensity of devotion as to be dissolved in tears, utterly absorbed in its mysteries and nourished with its fruits." Thomas' renown as a preacher quickly spread beyond university and monastery walls, and his sermons attracted enormous congregations.

In 1252 Thomas completed his Cologne studies, and at the age of twenty-seven was sent to the University of Paris to begin a program of study for a Masters of Theology. It was during this time that he met and became friends with a Franciscan student also studying at the University of Paris: St. Bonaventure, to whom the Catholic Church aptly refers as the "Seraphic Doctor". Thomas and Bonaventure would later become two of the greatest and most influential theologians of the Middle Ages, and their writings continue to bless Christianity.

It was a difficult, tense environment in Paris for the Dominicans and Franciscans at this time. Some of the secular and non-monastic clergy viewed these popular and eloquent mendicant orders as rivals, and well-orchestrated appeals were made to Rome and other Church authorities to forbid their influence at the university and, for that matter, the universal Church. These deliberate attacks would prove to be the worst crisis in the long history of the Order of Preachers.

Although Pope Innocent IV initially sided with the mendicant orders' opponents, he would soon die. He was succeeded by Pope Alexander IV, who proved to be friendly to the Dominican and Franciscan friars. He compelled the university to admit Thomas and Bonaventure to positions of teachers and doctors of theology. Thomas was given a license to teach and received his doctorate in theology in 1257 at the age of thirty-two, well below the established age for this unique honorary title and privilege. St. Dominic appeared to Thomas as he prayed before his inaugural address accepting this title, bidding him to take for his main text Psalm 103: "Watering the mountains from above, the earth will be filled with the fruit of your works." This Thomas did admirably, preaching a splendid account on the holy vocation of a theologian.

Biographers are uncertain where Aquinas was from 1259 to 1269. It is generally believed that the now renowned friar was in Italy at the request of his order, establishing a Dominican studium in Rome closely affiliated with the papal court. He is also believed to have lectured and preached during these years in many Italian towns and churches. The primary responsibility of a

Master in Theology in these houses of study was to write or speak on the meaning of Scripture and in formal disputations to address the speculative issues and theological problems of the time. The Rome Dominican house of studies was to be Thomas' "personal studium", and he was given ample time to pursue his own research and writing. This studium still exists in Rome today as the University of St. Thomas, commonly referred to as the Angelicum.

In 1263 Thomas would complete one of his famed works, the *Catena Aurea* (Golden Chain), which he compiled at the request of Pope Urban IV. This massive collection of thousands of direct quotes of the early Church Fathers on each of the four Gospels is a timeless monument to the sheer intellectual and spiritual brilliance of Thomas, who would often refer to this book in many of his later writings and sermons. He once stated, "I would rather have a copy of St. John Chrysostom on Matthew than the whole of Paris."

During these years in Italy Thomas also began and completed one of his more famous works, the *Summa Contra Gentiles*, which served as an apologetic text used by Catholic missionaries who were evangelizing the unbelievers of his time, particularly Muslims. It was Thomas' belief that effective Christian teachers should first and foremost be contemplatives who love and delight in the investigation of truth. In his view, the most successful approach to combating theological errors is an intense investigation of Catholic doctrine.

He was sent once again to the University of Paris in 1270 to occupy one of its two Dominican chairs of theology. During these final years in Paris, Thomas was to put considerable time and effort into perhaps his greatest and most important work: the *Summa Theologica*, or *Summary of Theology*, which he had actually started during his tenure in Italy. This book is essentially Thomas' own course in theology and is considered by many scholars as the crowning glory of the saintly friar. It is this masterpiece, along with *Summa Contra Gentiles*, that constitutes the fullest and most exact exposition of Catholic dogma the Church and world has ever known.

At the request of the Dominicans, Thomas returned to Rome in 1272 and was then sent from there to set up another studium and to lecture at the University of Naples, his home city. A year later, while he was saying Mass in the Dominican convent there, Thomas received a personal revelation so overwhelming that afterward he could never again write or dictate. Although the *Summa Theologica* was started over four years earlier, it was set aside and left incomplete. The world will never know the particular mystical experience and insights that were granted Thomas during this particular Mass, but afterward he stated, "The end of my labors is come. All that I have written seems to me so much straw after the things that have been revealed to me." Those are striking words from arguably one of the world's greatest minds, especially in light of his never-ending quest and thirst for truth. The mind, heart, and soul of the "Angelic Doctor", as the Church would later call him, could never rest on anything but the eternal Truth.

To Thomas the ultimate purpose and goal of theology was not just the acquisition of knowledge, but God Himself. It is a great thing to know about God, but a far greater thing to know and love Him in actuality. The perfection of contemplation to this great Dominican was the intellectual and spiritual apprehension of the nature and person of the Holy Trinity. This led to the effective imparting of that knowledge to others. "It is better to enlighten", he once wrote, "than merely to shine." It seems that our Lord rewarded His faithful Dominican servant with the ultimate quest of his life: God Himself. St. Paul once wrote, "Eye has not seen and ear has not heard, nor has it so much as dawned on man what God has prepared for those who love Him" (1 Cor. 2:9). One can surmise that Thomas was given the unique mystical privilege of experiencing a glimpse of the supernatural reality of the Eternal.

Up to this point in his life Thomas enjoyed good health, but then his health quickly failed. Although quite ill and finding it difficult to travel, the ailing friar was summoned by the Pope to attend the Second Council at Lyons. The main business of this gathering of Catholic bishops was to discuss the reunion of the Eastern and Western Churches, and Thomas was to bring with him his treatise *Against the Errors of the Greeks*. He did not make the council. The weak friar fell seriously ill on the way and was brought to a nearby Cistercian monastery at Fossa Nova, where the monks ministered to him. Thomas died at this monastery a month later. As the monks brought the dying friar the Blessed Sacrament, he addressed his Lord stating, "I receive You, price of my soul's redemption, I receive You, viaticum for my pilgrimage, for whose love I have studied, kept watch and labored and preached and taught."

The intellectual light of the thirteenth century passed away on March 7, 1274, at the age of forty-nine. St. Albert the Great, his old Dominican master, although far away in Cologne, suddenly burst into tears in the midst of his religious community and exclaimed, "Brother Thomas Aquinas, my son in Christ, the light of the Church, is dead! God has revealed it to me!"

Thomas' doctrine and teachings were studied by Dominican students over the ensuing years in the form of isolated extracts and selected questions. In 1309 the Dominicans formally embraced Aquinas' teachings as the official doctrine of the order. Pope John XXII officially launched the investigation into the writings and personal holiness of Thomas in 1318 and five years later declared him a saint. The same Pope commended the Dominicans and stated that "after the apostles and Doctors of the early Church, Thomas was the teacher who most enlightened the Church".

In 1367 the Dominicans translated his body with great pomp to Toulouse, France, where it still lies today in the Church of St. Servin. Three hundred years later the title Doctor of the Church was conferred on St. Thomas Aquinas by Pope Pius V. In 1880 Pope Leo XIII declared him patron of all academics, Catholic universities, colleges, and schools. Officially confirming him as the greatest theologian of the Catholic Church, the Pope stated in an encyclical: "Reason, reared aloft on the wings of St. Thomas, could scarcely soar higher, and it is almost impossible even for faith to be supported by additional or stronger aids from reason than has been furnished by the Angelic Doctor." In more recent times Pope John Paul II, who as a young priest studied at the Angelicum in Rome, spoke on the teachings of the Angelic Doctor, saying, "The humanism of St. Thomas pivots around this essential intuition: Man comes from God and to Him he must return. Time is the realm in which he can fulfill his noble mission." John Paul II encouraged Christians to study the thought of

St. Thomas, who, "with his firm confidence in reason, is able to harmonize nature and grace".

The written legacy of St. Thomas Aquinas, as seen in the twenty or more volumes of his works, is a monumental tribute to the sheer intellectual and spiritual genius of perhaps Christianity's greatest philosopher and theologian. It remains to be seen if any soul has ever been so gifted as St. Thomas Aquinas to be able to understand, process, organize, and lucidly harmonize virtually all the available knowledge of his time in the fields of philosophy, theology, the sciences, and human nature as thoroughly and doctrinally sound as this humble and pious Dominican friar. Although a forty-nine-year life span is relatively short, the impressive number of writings and range of topics tackled by Thomas points to a man who was driven on an intellectual journey to all aspects of truth. Writing, preaching, and teaching was a never-ending passion that was the fabric of his life. Throughout his adult life Thomas either penned his own writings or dictated to fellow friars. These dictations also demonstrate the remarkable genius of Thomas, who sometimes simultaneously dictated different things to different friars. He was even known to dictate in his sleep.

As a philosopher, the greatest contribution of Aquinas was his ability to incorporate the works of Aristotle with the building up of an ordered and systematic presentation of Catholic doctrine. Thomas presented much of his thought and teaching in a consistent, orderly fashion of (1) stating a problem or question; (2) objectively and fairly singling out arguments against his own point of view; (3) stating his position with arguments to support it; and (4) one by one, answering the objections of his opponents. His writing in this format contained ample support from biblical sources, the early Church Fathers and other notable saints, former Church councils, and the world's great philosophers.

Perhaps no single text reflects his supreme wisdom more vividly than the *Summa Theologica*, which is more than two thousand double-columned pages long, containing thirty-eight tracts, 631 questions, and more than three thousand articles. Over 10,000 objections to Thomas' position are addressed. Aquinas interwove within this great work references to nineteen Catholic councils, forty-one popes, fifty-two Fathers of the Church, and hundreds of classical philosophers such as Plato and Aristotle, not to mention countless quotes from Scripture. To call this effort a monumental task is an understatement, especially when this *Summa* was considered by Thomas as an *introductory* book of theology.

In the mind of Thomas there could never be a contradiction between revealed faith and reason, as both come from the one source of all truth—God, the One and Absolute Truth. Three centuries after his death at the Council of Trent the teachings of Thomas were formally laid down before the assembly as one of the main authoritative sources of Catholic Faith. With the single exception of St. Augustine, no other theologian has had so much influence on the Western Church.

Thomas' contributions to the Christian world were not limited to the fields of dogma, apologetics, and philosophy. Some of the world's most beautiful prayers and sacred songs were penned by Aquinas, and their doctrinal accuracy and tenderness of feeling are reflections of the immense knowledge and love he had for God. Thomas had a particular fondness and intimate devotion for the Mass and to Jesus Christ in the Holy Eucharist.

When Pope Urban IV instituted the Feast of Corpus Christi, he asked Thomas to compose the liturgical office and Mass for this solemn celebration. To this day some of these prayers are still recited in the Mass of Corpus Christi, the Body and Blood of Christ.

St. Thomas may be best known as a great intellect and Christian thinker, but his holy life was equally impressive. Although graced with such an incredible mastery of knowledge, in his personal life he exemplified a simple, reserved, humble servant of God. He was known to rise early in the morning, with the usual practice of going to confession, saying Mass, then immediately attending another Mass. The rest of his day he normally spent reading, praying, writing, and teaching. Thomas liked to go often to a church and spend quiet time there with Jesus in the tabernacle. His heart was drawn like a magnet to prayer whenever confronted with a theological or intellectual question that challenged him. God once revealed to St. Catherine of Siena, the great fourteenth-century Dominican Doctor and mystic, that "*Thomas learned more from prayer than from study.*" Since he had a profound devotion to Mass and the Holy Eucharist, and it was not uncommon for his Dominican brethren to find him so deeply moved and absorbed during the service that he would stop, needing to be roused to continue. The sacredness of the Mass and his corresponding love of God simply overwhelmed him.

All those who knew Thomas found him to be considerate, kind, and patient with other people. He exhibited no trace of vanity or pride, so often found in those with great intellectual ability or personal achievements. Friendship, according to Thomas, is the greatest model for understanding and learning charity. He was never known to lose his temper, even in the midst of heated disputations, and never uttered anything unkind or humiliating to those opposing his views.

The personal sanctity found in Thomas was primarily centered in his intellectual service of God and the Catholic Church, rather than in extraordinary supernatural miracles often noted in the lives of other saints. During the process of investigating Thomas' life it was argued that there was such a lack of documented miracles that he was not a good candidate for canonization. Pope John XXII, however, staunchly defended Thomas, stating, "Every question he answered was a miracle."

We do, however, have some accounts witnessed by others that most definitely indicate that St. Thomas' life was indeed not only that of a great thinker, but of an extraordinarily holy man. Notable among these is the account of a Church sacristan in Naples. Thomas had just completed an important work explaining the transubstantiation of Christ in the Eucharist, and the sacristan claimed to have seen Thomas place the completed book on the altar. While Thomas was raised in mystical levitation above the ground, absorbed in prayer, the voice of Christ was heard from the crucifix in front of him, saying, "Thomas, you have written well of me; what reward will you take from me for your labors?" to which the friar responded, "Lord, nothing except You."

> *"God cannot in any way be deficient in goodness. For what is essential to a being cannot be lacking. . . . It is impossible for God not to be good. We can use a more appropriate example to illustrate this: as it is impossible for a man not to be a man, so it is impossible for God not to be perfectly good."*
> —St. Thomas Aquinas

THE
JOYFUL
MYSTERIES

THE FIRST JOYFUL MYSTERY

THE ANNUNCIATION OF OUR LORD

Humility

Whoever humbles himself like this child, he is the greatest in the kingdom of heaven.—Matthew 18:4

Whatever we are able to do He gave us the power to do when He created us. (H 11)

Seek praises from God alone. (H 10)

Humility orders us in relation to God; Justice regulates us in regard to our neighbors; and Purity with regard to ourselves. (H 17)

The Devil takes away the seed of good works, at the same time that he makes men to glory in them. (H 40)

Man has to believe others in matters that he cannot know perfectly by himself. Now no one is to be believed as much as God is. Thus, those who will not believe the statements of faith are not wise, but foolish and proud.

(C 9)

If you seek an example of humility, look on the Crucified. Although He was God, He chose to be judged by
Pontius Pilate and to suffer death.... The Master chose
to die for His servant; the Life of the Angels suffered
death for man. (C 45)

Humility is the road to exaltation. (C 61)

True humility consists in not presuming on our own
strength, but in trusting to obtain all things from the
power of God. (C 106)

Of all the signs of a man's knowledge and wisdom, none
is proof of greater wisdom than that he does not cling to
his own opinion.... For those who cling to their own
judgment so as to mistrust others and trust in themselves
alone invariably prove themselves fools and are judged
as such. (C 129)

Our Lord will hold to what He promised to the humble, when He will exalt them in the same measure that
they had been abased and disdained; and to what He
promised to the proud, when He will humble them as
much as they had glorified themselves. (W 48)

In dispensing His favors God does not consider men's
power, strength, riches, or physical beauty.... It is above
all people of humble condition who progress in the
Church of God and abound in spiritual graces. (W 52)

God alone is His own goodness and He alone is essentially good. All other creatures are said to be good according as they participate, to some extent, in Him. (SS 123)

Man does not know the hour of his death. (SS 319)

See now the aid which God gives a man by His correction, how necessary it is, that you may know that however much you may be corrected by men, if the grace of God is not present and calling within you, that correction is worthless. (T 3)

It would be of no advantage to ascend in status if a man did not also grow in merit. (T 9)

In this world a man sometimes obtains earthly goods by contentiousness and deceit, but heavenly riches are obtained by meekness.... *Blessed are the meek: for they shall possess the land.* (T 21)

Natural reason tells us that because of the inadequacies we perceive in ourselves we need to subject ourselves to some superior source of help and direction; and whatever that source might be, everybody calls it *God.* (SP xxv)

Nature can't exist without God's activity: it would fall away to nothing unless God's power maintained it in existence, as Augustine makes clear. So nature can't act without God's activity. (SP 299)

Earthly greatness is confounded when heavenly greatness shows itself. (CA 69)

What avails noble birth to him whose life is disgrace-
ful? Or, on the other hand, what hurt is a low origin to
him who has the luster of virtue? (CA 100)

Since man's nature is dependent on a higher nature, natural knowledge does not suffice for its perfection, and
some supernatural knowledge is necessary. (ST 1181)

There is only one nobility, to do the will of God. Therefore it follows, *Whosoever shall do the will of my Father
which is in Heaven, the same is my brother, and sister, and
mother.* (CA 477)

When human frailty beset with difficulties considers the
weakness of its own powers, it looks upon itself as in
darkness; when it raises its view to the protection of
Heaven, it straightway beholds the rise of the morning
star, which give its light. (CA 545)

Men are subject to many failings, so that he who is
superior in one respect, is or may be inferior in another.
(ST 1321)

*Whosoever shall humble himself as this little child, the same
is the greatest in the kingdom of heaven*; for by how much a
man is humble now, by so much shall he be exalted in
the kingdom of heaven. (CA 623)

High place courts him who flies from it, and shuns him who courts it. A better life then, and not a more worthy degree, should be our object. (CA 696)

So it is with all holy men, they love to be not where sumptuous banquets are, but where holiness flourishes. (CA 716–17)

Discord, whereby a man holds to his own way of thinking, and departs from that of others, is reckoned to be a daughter of vainglory. (ST 1353)

Without grace it is impossible to avoid sins. (ST 2617)

Notwithstanding the uncertainty of death, the uncertainty of the judgment conduces to watchfulness. (ST 2937)

Exaltation in this life does not lessen the reward of the other life, except for him who seeks his own glory from that exaltation: whereas he who turns that exaltation to the profit of others acquires thereby a reward for himself. (ST 2992)

Life is God's gift to man, and is subject to His power. . . . The passage from this life to another and happier one is subject not to man's free-will but to the power of God. (ST 1469)

Natural reason tells man that he is subject to a higher being, on account of the defects which he perceives in himself, and in which he needs help and direction from someone above him. (ST 1555)

If we obtain something from God through His eternal will, it is due, not to our merits, but to His goodness. (ST 1587)

Those who represent themselves as being greater than they are, are a source of annoyance to others, since they seem to wish to surpass others: whereas those who make less account of themselves are a source of pleasure, since they seem to defer to others by their moderation. (ST 1663)

Humility makes us honor others and esteem them better than ourselves, in so far as we see some of God's gifts in them. (ST 1730)

Pride is accounted the common mother of all sins. (ST 1813)

To fall away from reverence for Him is the first part of pride. (ST 1843)

God alone is perfect.... Humility, considered as a special virtue, regards chiefly the subjection of man to God. (ST 1848)

It is contrary to humility to aim at greater things through confiding is one's own powers: but to aim at greater things through confidence in God's help, is not contrary to humility; especially since the more one subjects oneself to God, the more is one exalted in God's sight. (ST 1849)

We may consider two things in man, namely that which is God's, and that which is man's. Whatever pertains to defect is man's: but whatever pertains to man's welfare and perfection is God's. (ST 1850)

Without falsehood one may avow and believe oneself in all ways unprofitable and useless in respect of one's own capability, so as to refer all one's sufficiency to God. (ST 1853)

Nature is not sufficient, and grace is necessary. (ST 1897)

Grace is caused in man by the presence of the God-head, as light in the air by the presence of the sun. (ST 2075)

The angel who announced Christ's birth did not go to Jerusalem, nor did he seek the Scribes and Pharisees, for they were corrupted, and full of ill-will. But the shepherds were single-minded, and were like the patriarchs and Moses in their mode of life. (ST 2213)

The profit which accrues to men from Christ is chiefly through faith and humility. (ST 2230)

Christ wished to be tempted; first that He might strengthen us against temptations ... second, that we might be warned, so that none, however holy, may think himself safe or free from temptation. (ST 2240)

The Second Joyful Mystery

The Visitation to Elizabeth

Love of Neighbor

You shall love your neighbor as yourself.
—Mark 12:31

It is the law of God that the things which we are unwilling should be done to us, we should not do to others; but that which we should wish to be done to us, that we should do to others. (H 69–70)

He who does almsgiving obtains three good gifts—(1) temporal good; (2) spiritual good; (3) eternal good. (H 85)

Leaves without flowers: these are they which have words without works. (H 102)

We ought to repay Him [God] by giving alms to the poor. (H 145)

We imitate God by being merciful, because mercy is bound to accompany love: "*Be ye merciful.*" And this must be in deed. (C 111)

By patience a brother may be won back again. (H 126)

We owe our neighbor two things: (1) Love. We owe our neighbor love, because he is our brother, seeing that we are God's children. ... (2) Reverence. We owe our neighbor reverence, because he is a child of God: "*Have we not all one Father?*" (C 112)

The good of our neighbor is advanced by things pertaining to the spiritual welfare of the soul rather than by things pertaining to the supplying of bodily needs, in proportion to the excellence of spiritual over corporal things. ... Spiritual works of mercy surpass corporal works of mercy. (ST 1996)

We should, on the contrary, forget the offenses of our enemy, even though he neither repents nor amends, in imitation of Christ who prayed for those who crucified Him, and who, far from repenting, mocked Him. ... For the height of perfection is to love our enemies, and to pray for them as did the Lord Jesus. (W 28–29)

One must, as St. Gregory said, honor man because he is man and made in the image and likeness of God, and not for anything that surrounds him (like riches, precious clothing, power, a noble name, or a multitude of friends and relations). (W 53)

One man should draw another to God's service. (ST 2014)

He who looks on himself as a son of God, ought, among other things, to imitate our Lord especially in His love. ... God's love is not restricted to any individual, but embraces all in common; for God loves "all things that are," as is said in Wisdom 11:24. Most of all He loves men. (SS 341)

He who loves goes out from himself, in so far as he wills the good of his friend and works for it. (T 287)

Love embraces two lives; active in the love of our neighbor, contemplative in the love of God. (CA 19)

Nothing so likens you to God, as to forgive him who has injured you. (CA 238)

He does not say, "Do not cause a sinner to cease," but do not judge; that is, be not a bitter judge; correct him indeed, but not as an enemy seeking revenge, but as a physician applying a remedy. (CA 264)

God looks more to the pious mind of the giver, than to the abundance of the thing given. (CA 402)

Let a man gently reprove whatever is in his power; what is not so let him bear with patience, and mourn over with affection, until He from above shall correct and heal, and let him defer till harvest-time to root out the tares and winnow the chaff. (CA 499)

Now sinners do not cease to be men, for sin does not destroy nature. Therefore we ought to love sinners out of charity. (ST 1290)

Peace is the *work of justice* indirectly, in so far as justice removes the obstacles to peace: but it is the work of charity directly, since charity, according to its very nature, causes peace. For love is a unitive force. (ST 1316)

If any man loves not his neighbor, neither does he love God. (ST 1296)

Of all the virtues which relate to our neighbor, mercy is the greatest, even as its act surpasses all others. . . . The sum total of the Christian religion consists in mercy, as regards external works. (ST 1320)

The reproof of the sinner, as to the exercise of the act of reproving, seems to imply the severity of justice, but, as to the intention of the reprover, who wishes to free a man from the evil of sin, it is an act of mercy and loving kindness. . . . *"Better are the wounds of a friend, than the deceitful kisses of an enemy."* (ST 1325–26)

Spiritual almsdeeds hold the first place. . . . The spirit is more excellent than the body, wherefore, even as a man in looking at himself, ought to look to his soul more than to his body, so ought he in looking after his neighbor, whom he ought to love as himself. (ST 1326)

We are bound to give alms of our surplus, as also to give alms to one whose need is extreme. (ST 1328)

The object both of charity and of envy is our neighbor's good, but by contrary movements, since charity rejoices in our neighbor's good, while envy grieves over it. (ST 1351)

In saving another, salvation is gained for ourselves also.

(CA 635)

None should despair of his neighbor, even though he see him lying in vices; because he knows not the riches of the Divine mercy. (CA 686)

Is it not better to have to answer for mercy than for severity? . . . Do you seek thereby the character of sanctity? Be strict in ordering your own life, in that of others lenient; let men hear of you as enjoining little, and performing much. (CA 770)

He whose duty it is to teach should not teach what is contrary to the truth. . . . The act itself of teaching is one of the spiritual almsdeeds. (ST 1372)

The love of God is the end to which the love of neighbor is directed. . . . God is loved in our neighbor. (ST 1375)

The reason why we ought to love others out of charity is because they are nigh to us, both as to the natural image of God, and as to the capacity for glory. (ST 1378)

He that seeks the good of the many, seeks in consequence his own good. . . . The individual good is impossible without the common good of the family, state, or kingdom. (ST 1395)

When a man hates or despises another, or is angry with or envious of him, he is led by slight indications to think evil of him, because everyone easily believes what he desires. . . . Suspicion denotes a certain amount of vice, and the further it goes, the more vicious it is. (ST 1448)

He who interprets doubtful matter for the best, may happen to be deceived more often than not; yet it is better to err frequently through thinking well of a wicked man, than to err less frequently through having an evil opinion of a good man. (ST 1449)

We must presume good of everyone, unless there be proof of the contrary. (ST 2727)

The life of righteous men preserves and forwards the common good, since they are the chief part of the community. Therefore it is in no way lawful to slay the innocent. (ST 1470)

It is unlawful to do a person harm, except by way of punishment in the cause of justice. (ST 1474)

A backbiter more and more loves and believes what he says, and consequently more and more hates his neighbor, and thus his knowledge of the truth becomes less and less. (ST 1506)

A friend is better than honor, and to be loved is better than to be honored. . . . A good name is a disposition for friendship. (ST 1508)

Man easily offends in words. (ST 1580)

Parting with money by giving it to others proceeds from a greater virtue than when we spend it on ourselves.
(ST 1683)

Clemency denotes a certain smoothness or sweetness of soul, whereby one is inclined to mitigate punishment. . . . The hardness of heart, which makes one ready to increase punishment, belongs to cruelty. (ST 1845)

Whatsoever things lead a man to inordinate self-esteem lead him to pride: and one of those is the observing of other people's failings. (ST 1857)

It is possible, by the acts of all the moral virtues, for one to direct one's neighbor to good by example. (ST 1940)

The good of the many should be preferred to the good of the individual. (ST 1962)

The salvation of the multitude is to be preferred to the peace of any individuals whatsoever. Consequently, when certain ones, by their perverseness, hinder the salvation of the multitude, the preacher and teacher should not fear to offend those men, in order that he may insure the salvation of the multitude. (ST 2247)

Man is induced to be merciful by the example of Divine mercy. (ST 2538)

Just as the fire acts with greater force on what is near than on what is distant, so too, charity loves with greater fervor those who are united to us than those who are far removed. (ST 1310)

When we pray we ought to ask for what we ought to desire. Now we ought to desire good things not only for ourselves, but also for others: for this is essential to the love which we owe to our neighbor. . . . Charity requires us to pray for others. (ST 1542)

THE THIRD JOYFUL MYSTERY

THE BIRTH OF JESUS

Spirit of Poverty

Blessed are the poor in spirit, for theirs is the kingdom of heaven.—Matthew 5:3

Temporal riches do not avail for the salvation of man in the day of judgment. (H 129)

Eternal riches are to be sought for three reasons: (1) on account of their truth, for they are true riches . . . (2) on account of their joyousness . . . (3) on account of eternity: "But the just shall live for evermore." (H 131)

None need be fearful of poverty who have acquired the riches of wisdom. (H 130)

The riches of this world are not true riches. . . . The crowns of the saints are to be earnestly sought for. (H 159)

The saints live not after the fashion of the world. . . . The dignity of the saints is so great because they are not of this world, but "of the household of God." (H 188)

In this life no man can fulfill his desires, nor can any creature satisfy a man's craving, for God alone satisfies and infinitely surpasses man's desire, which for that reason is never at rest except in God. (C 96)

Take note that whatever man seeks in this world, he will find it more perfect and more excellent in God alone. If you seek delight, you will find supreme delight in God. . . . Do you seek wealth? You will find in Him all you desire in abundance. (C 127)

He made man for a certain purpose; but not for the sake of material pleasures, since dumb animals have them, but that he may have eternal life. For it is the Lord's will that man have eternal life. (C 131)

There are some who are never satisfied with what they have and always want more. This is lack of moderation, since desire should always be measured according to one's needs: "Give me neither beggary nor riches; give me but the necessities of life." (C 139)

There are some who are worried from day to day about temporal matters as much as a year in advance. Those who are so concerned are never at rest. . . . Hence our Lord teaches us to ask that our bread be given us *today*, i.e., whatever we need for the present. (C 140)

Our natural life is as nothing compared to the life of grace. (C 203)

The world tempts man by awakening in him an excessive and unbridled desire for earthly goods. For this
reason, the Apostle says that "the desire of money is the
root of all evils." (C 152–53)

To increase our love, we are commanded to keep holy
the Sabbath. . . . Man always tends downward toward
earthly things unless he takes means to raise himself above
them. It is indeed necessary to have a certain time for
this. (C 190)

We should sacrifice our possessions by giving alms. (C 195)

The desires of man are never satisfied, because the heart
of man is made for God. Thus says St. Augustine: "Thou
hast made us for Thee, O Lord, and our heart is restless
until it rests in Thee." . . . Thus, nothing less than God
can satisfy the human heart. (C 242)

The more one covets, the less one loves. (C 243)

I ask that from the abundance of Your immense generosity You may bestow that which is needed to cure
my illness, to wash away my uncleanness, to illuminate
my blindness, to enrich my poverty, and to clothe my
nakedness. (P 73 and 75)

As the world or God predominate in a man's heart, he
must be drawn contrary ways; for God draws him who
serves Him to things above; the earth draws to things
beneath. (CA 248)

We must heed the order of desire, as regulated by charity, so that a corresponding order of goods to be hoped and asked for from God may be established. The order of charity requires us to love God above all things. And so charity moves our first desire in the direction of the things that are of God. (ss 347)

Happiness is not to be found in material goods [because] such goods cannot satisfy man. This is clear on many scores. . . . Material goods, as being the lowest in the order of nature, do not contain all goodness but possess only a portion of goodness. (ss 353–54)

Man naturally desires perpetual stability. But this cannot be found in material things, which are subject to corruption and many kinds of change. Therefore the human appetite cannot find the sufficiency it needs in material goods. Accordingly, man's ultimate happiness cannot consist in such goods. (ss 354)

The ultimate good . . . contains perpetual and full joy. Our Lord was thinking of this when He bade us, in John 16:24: "Ask and you shall receive, that your joy may be full." Full joy, however, can be gained from no creature, but only from God, in whom the entire plentitude of goodness resides. (ss 362)

What, then, do you possess in possessing God? I say that in possessing God you possess what is in God. And what is in God? Glory and riches. (w 20)

All things pass away like a shadow. . . . Find among earthly things that which will remain, that which will satisfy desire, and I will admit to you that blessedness is there; but it cannot be found. Wrongly, therefore, do they think that blessedness is in earthly things. (W 17–18)

The saints have God as their possession, and He is sufficient for them. (W 20)

If [people] had perfect faith they would live as about to depart from this world soon, not as to possess it for ever. (CA 70)

Whatever confers blessedness, that is the chief good.
(CA 147)

They must be esteemed to have lost their sense, who either pursuing abundance, or fearing lack of temporal goods, lose those which are eternal. (CA 161)

Because wealth is not ours but God's, God would have us stewards of His wealth, and not lords. (CA 202)

Human reason is very deficient in things concerning God. A sign of this is that philosophers in their researches, by natural investigation, into human affairs, have fallen into many errors, and have disagreed among themselves. . . . It was necessary for Divine matters to be delivered to them by way of faith, being told to them, as it were, by God Himself Who cannot lie. (ST 1182)

Eternal salvation takes precedence of temporal good. (ST 1227)

The soul that is a deserter from God, must necessarily turn to other things. (ST 1260)

We ought not to place our treasure in that which passes away, but in that which abides forever. Which then is better? To place it on earth where its security is doubtful, or in Heaven where it will be certainly preserved? (CA 243–44)

That treasure *in which are hidden all the treasures of wisdom and knowledge,* is either God the Word, who seems hid in Christ's Flesh, or the Holy Scriptures. . . . Be rich in the knowledge of God. (CA 513)

If you should reign over the whole world, you would not be able to buy your soul; whence it follows, *Or what shall a man give in exchange for his soul?* (CA 595)

Spiritual things infinitely surpass corporal things. (ST 1327)

To have riches is no sin; but moderation is to be observed. (CA 669)

Like the hired laborer looks first to his task, and after to his daily food, so ought we to mind first those things which concern the glory of God, then those which concern our own profit. (CA 679)

Our Passover is celebrated when we leave the things of the earth, and hasten to the things of heaven. (CA 874)

Covetousness is said to be idolatry on account of a certain likeness of bondage, because both the covetous and the idolater serve the creature rather than the Creator. . . . Unbelief corrupts the intellect whereas covetousness corrupts the affections. (ST 2789)

The rich man is reproved for deeming external things to belong to him principally, as though he had not received them from another, namely from God. (ST 1476)

A man's good name takes precedence of wealth because it is more akin to spiritual goods, wherefore it is written (Prov. 22:1): *A good name is better than great riches.* (ST 1505)

It is not possible to pay God as much as we owe Him. (ST 1532)

We should seek temporal things not in the first but in the second place. (ST 1542)

When our mind is intent on temporal things in order that it may rest in them, it remains immersed therein; but when it is intent on them in relation to the acquisition of beatitude, it is not lowered by them, but raises them to a higher level. (ST 1542)

By reason of his not being a lover of money, it follows that a man readily makes use of it, whether for himself, or for the good of others, or for God's glory. Thus it derives a certain excellence from being useful in many ways. (ST 1685)

Lust for riches, properly speaking, brings darkness on the soul, when it puts out the light of charity, by preferring the love of riches to the love of God. (ST 1688)

The covetous man is not easily cured. . . . The covetous man profits neither others nor himself, since he does not even use his own goods for his own profit. (ST 1694)

Just as He took upon Himself the death of the body in order to bestow spiritual life on us, so did He bear bodily poverty, in order to enrich us spiritually. (ST 2238)

The more lowly He seemed by reason of His poverty, the greater might the power of His Godhead be shown to be. . . . For this reason did He choose a poor maid for His Mother, a poorer birthplace; for this reason did He live in want. Learn this from the manger. (ST 2239)

Not all solicitude about temporal things is forbidden, but that which is superfluous and inordinate. . . . We ask God for them in the sense that they may be granted us in so far as they are expedient for salvation. (ST 1542)

The Fourth Joyful Mystery

The Presentation in the Temple

Obedience

If you love me, you will keep my commandments.
—John 14:15

We ought to avoid a thoughtless choice. . . . Submit all choice to Christ as the Judge. (H 10)

Righteousness is a right will. (H 98)

"No man can serve two masters" (Matt. 6:24). The Lord Jesus Christ shows in these words that God alone is to be served, and that no one is to be obeyed in opposition to God. (H 120)

We ought to serve God because He alone has in us the right of possession, as being the true Lord. . . . To serve God is to reign. (H 121)

There is no master able to teach all things save Our Lord Jesus Christ: "All wisdom is from the Lord God, and hath been always with Him, and is before all time" (Sir. 1:1). (H 147)

Obey God immediately.... We ought to obey the call of God "straightaway." (H 191)

The devil tempts us to disobey God and to refuse to be subject to Him. This temptation is removed by faith, since faith teaches us that He is the Lord of all, which is why we must obey Him. (C 7)

Those who obey kings rather than God, in matters where they ought not to obey them, make kings their gods: "We ought to obey God rather than men." (C 15)

We must conduct ourselves according to the purpose for which God made us, seeing that He made man to preside over all the things on earth and to be subject to Himself. Accordingly, we must rule and hold dominion over the things of the earth, but we must be subject to God by obeying and serving Him, and so we shall attain to the enjoyment of God. (C 21)

He atoned to God the Father for sin, for which man himself was unable to atone. Christ's charity and obedience were greater than the sin and disobedience of the first man. (C 41)

If you seek an example of obedience, follow Him who was made obedient to the Father even unto death.... "By the obedience of one, many shall be made just."

(C 45)

The Holy Spirit helps us (and to a certain extent compels us) to keep the Commandments. For no one can keep the Commandments unless he loves God: "If any man loves Me, he will keep My word." (C 74)

We learn from the Holy Spirit (by His gift of knowledge) to do not our own but God's will, and by virtue of this gift we pray to God that His will may be done on earth as it is in Heaven. It is in this that the gift of knowledge is proved. (C 130)

We should ask nothing of God but that His will be done in our regard (in other words, that His will be fulfilled in us). For man's heart is right when it agrees with the divine will. (C 130)

We owe God that which we take away from His right, and God's right is that we do His will in preference to our own. Hence, we deprive God of His right when we prefer our own will to His, and this is sin. (C 143–44)

Human law judges deeds and words, but divine law also judges thoughts. This is because human laws are made by men, who see things only exteriorly, but divine law is from God, who sees both external things and the very interior of men. (C 241)

Nothing is more suitable to man than to imitate his Creator, and to carry out, to the degree that he is able, the will of God. (W 3)

Last and above all, let us take tender care of God Him-self, doing everywhere and always that which He most desires us to do and that for which He has particularly destined us. (w 60)

Perfect attachment of the will to God is brought about by love and by grace, whereby man is justified, accord-ing to Romans 3:24: "Being justified freely by His grace." For man is made just by union with God through love.

(SS 253–54)

O merciful God, grant that I may desire ardently, search prudently, recognize truly, and bring to perfect comple-tion whatever is pleasing to You for the praise and glory of Your name. . . . Bestow upon me the power to accom-plish Your will, as is necessary and fitting for the salva-tion of my soul. (P 5)

It is just that we should be subject to God. The highest perfection of a thing is that it should be subject to that which perfects it. (T 17)

The light of natural reason, whereby we discern what is good and what is evil, which is the function of the nat-ural law, is nothing else than an imprint on us of the divine light. It is therefore evident that the natural law is nothing else than the rational creature's participation of the eternal law. (T 85)

Eternal law can't make a mistake but reason can. So, in giving consent to human reason, will is not always right, and not always giving consent to eternal law. In moral action, just as in logical reasoning, a fault early on will lead to others. (SP 372)

Because to be right and good a thing must measure up to its proper standard, human willing, to be good, must conform to God's willing. (SP 377)

By obedience knowledge is increased. (CA 29)

We are bound to do many things which we cannot do without the aid of healing grace, such as to love God and our neighbor, and likewise to believe the articles of faith. But with the help of grace we can do this. (ST 1183)

Things that are necessary for salvation come under the precepts of the Divine law. (ST 1189)

It is therefore essential to charity that man should so love God as to wish to submit to Him in all things, and always to follow the rule of His commandments; since whatever is contrary to His commandments is manifestly contrary to charity, and therefore by its very nature is capable of destroying charity. (ST 1285)

They seem not to know God who do not serve Him worthily. (CA 289)

The precepts of the Divine law do not bind less than those of the natural law: wherefore, just as no dispensation is possible from the natural law, so neither can there be from positive Divine law. (ST 2591)

God is satisfied if we accomplish what we can. Nevertheless justice tends to make man repay God as much as he can, by subjecting his mind to Him entirely. (ST 1432)

The natural law, considered in itself, has the same force at all times and places. . . . The law of nature is imprinted on the heart. (ST 2810)

It belongs to the order of justice that a man should obey his superior in those matters to which the rights of his authority extend. (ST 1490)

Man is master of his own actions but not those of others. (ST 1587)

All acts of virtue, in so far as they come under a precept, belong to obedience. . . . Obedience is said to ingraft and protect all virtues. (ST 1643)

The law of the Gospel is the law of love. . . . The Divine Law instructs man perfectly about such things as are necessary for right living. (ST 1657 and 1761)

Human judgment should conform to the Divine judgment, when this is manifest. (ST 1660)

Man's reason is right, in so far as it is ruled by the Divine will, the first and supreme rule. (ST 1817)

In spiritual things there is a twofold servitude and a twofold freedom: for there is the servitude of sin and the servitude of justice; and there is likewise a twofold freedom, from sin, and from justice. . . . Man, by his natural reason, is inclined to justice, while sin is contrary to natural reason. (ST 1949)

By obedience a man offers to God his will. (ST 1979)

Christ had most perfect obedience to God, according to Philippians 2:8: *Becoming obedient unto death.* And hence He taught nothing pertaining to merit which He did not fulfil more perfectly Himself. (ST 2067)

Christ, though not subject to the Law, wished, nevertheless, to submit to circumcision and the other burdens of the Law, in order to give an example of humility and obedience; and in order to show His approval of the Law. (ST 2222)

Obedience is preferred to all sacrifices, according to 1 Samuel 15:22: *Obedience is better than sacrifices.* Therefore it was fitting that the sacrifice of Christ's Passion and death should proceed from obedience. (ST 2279)

Human willing can't conform to God's willing by equaling it, but it can imitate it. And in the same way human knowing conforms to God's knowing by knowing truth. (SP 377)

The Fifth Joyful Mystery

The Finding of the Child Jesus
in the Temple

Piety

You . . . must be perfect as your heavenly Father is perfect.
—Matthew 5:48

By holiness of life man passes over and comes to his
heavenly city. (H 29)

A holy man is formed by charity—(1 Cor. 16:14), "Let
all your things be done with charity." (H 31)

We ought to walk in the light, as doing nothing worthy
of reproof. (H 51)

What can be more glorious than to be of God? . . . What
can be more unhappy than not to be of God? (H 57)

The steps in which we should follow Him are three—
(1) in the purity of innocence, . . . (2) in the firmness
of patience, . . . (3) in charity. . . . He who so follows
Him in these steps shall come to the joy of eternal
blessedness. (H 71)

It is evident that the just ever have Christ to dwell in their hearts. How great is the happiness of him who ever has Christ dwelling in his heart. (H 99)

Two things are needful for a man—*firstly*, interior perfection; *secondly*, exterior conversation: the former for his own sake, the latter for the sake of others. (H 176)

Two things are required in order to obtain eternal life: the grace of God and man's will. And although God made man without man's help, He does not sanctify him without his cooperation. (C 132)

We pray to Him to give us bread, that is to say, His Word. From this there arises in man the beatitude of hungering for righteousness, because the possession of spiritual goods increases our desire for them. This desire begets that hunger whose reward is the fullness of eternal life. (C 141)

Perfection for man consists in the love of God and of neighbor. The three Commandments on the first tablet pertain to the love of God; the seven on the second pertain to the love of neighbor. (C 199)

A long life is a full life, and it is not observed in time but in activity. . . . Life, however, is full inasmuch as it is a life of virtue. So a man who is virtuous and holy enjoys a long life even if in body he dies young. (C 203)

"Be ye perfect as your heavenly Father is perfect." Holy Scripture never orders and never counsels us to do the impossible. By these words, then, the Lord Jesus does not command us *to accomplish* the very works and ways of God, . . . but He invites us *to model ourselves* on them, as much as is possible, by applying ourselves to imitate them. We can do this with the help of grace and we should do so. (w 3)

The more the heart of man is expanded by the love of God and of his neighbor, and the more his meditations, his fervent prayers, his just aspirations, his humility, and his generosity have opened his soul to grace—the more elevated and greater is the grace that God the all-powerful will bestow upon him. (w 37)

At the Last Judgment the Lord will take no account of the person of kings and princes. He will judge with perfect equity the great and the lowly, and He will glorify each not according to his power, nobility, and beauty, but according to his humility and charity. (w 52-53)

The more a soul has been modeled on its Creator in this world, the more it will be like Him in the life to come; and the more it will be like Him, the greater will be its bliss, the more it will give glory to God, and the more it will be useful to every creature. (w 77)

The first thing necessary is faith, by which you may come to a knowledge of the truth. Secondly, hope is necessary, that your intention may be fixed on the right end. Thirdly, love is necessary, that your affections may be perfectly put in order. (ss 4)

The closer any creature draws to God, the more it shares in His goodness and the more abundantly it is filled with gifts infused by Him. Thus he who comes closer to a fire shares to a greater extent in its heat. (ss 257)

O Lord my God, make me submissive without protest, poor without discouragement, chaste without regret, patient without complaint, humble without posturing, cheerful without frivolity, mature without gloom, and quick-witted without flippancy. (p 9)

You Who are the source, the sustainer, and the rewarder of all virtues, grant that I may abide on the firm ground of faith, be sheltered by an impregnable shield of hope, and be adorned in the bridal garment of charity. (p 33)

Sons ought to be imitators of their parents. Therefore he who professes that God is his Father ought to try to be an imitator of God, by avoiding things that make him unlike God and by earnestly praying for those perfections that make him like to God. Hence we are commanded in Jeremiah 3:19: "Thou shalt call me *Father* and shalt not cease to walk after me." (ss 340)

Although God is said to be near to all men by reason of His special care over them, He is exceptionally close to the good who strive to draw near to Him in faith and love.... Indeed, He not only draws nigh to them; He even dwells in them through grace. (ss 345)

Among the various indications that make the holiness of God known to men, the most convincing sign is the holiness of men, who are sanctified by the divine indwelling. (SS 350)

Since man's natural desire always inclines toward his own good which consists in some perfection, the consequence is that as long as something remains to be desired, man has not yet reached his final perfection. (SS 352)

Happiness is the ultimate perfection of man.... Consequently man's ultimate perfection and final good consist in union with God, according to Psalm 72:28: "It is good for me to adhere to my God." (SS 355)

The study of the soul is exceedingly useful for the study of all the truth embodied in other sciences. For indeed it gives great scope to the other parts of philosophy. (T 59)

The ultimate perfection of the human intellect is the divine truth: and other truths perfect the intellect in relation to the divine truth. (T 204)

In so far as he is a contemplative, man becomes more than a man.... Contemplation does not consist principally in this life, but in the life to come. (T 224-25)

Good use of our freedom to choose is said to be virtue.... For the activity of virtue is nothing else than good use of one's freedom to choose. (SP 392)

Faith, hope and charity are the foundation of all virtues; those that follow are like additions over and above them. (CA 23)

To follow Him ought to be preferred to all occupations. (CA 136)

Many measuring the commandments of God by their own weakness, not by the strength of the saints, hold these commandments for impossible.... Christ enjoins not impossibilities but perfection. (CA 206)

Be ye then perfect, as your Father which is in Heaven is perfect.... As our sons after the flesh resemble their fathers in some part of their bodily shape, so do spiritual sons resemble their father God, in holiness. (CA 210)

The sum of all Christian discipline is comprehended in mercy and piety. (CA 214)

To believe does indeed depend on the will of the believer: but man's will needs to be prepared by God with grace, in order that he may be raised to things which are above his nature. (ST 1201)

A wise man in any branch of knowledge is one who knows the highest cause of that kind of knowledge, and is able to judge of all matters by that cause: and a wise man *absolutely*, is one who knows the cause which is absolutely highest, namely God. Hence the knowledge of Divine things is called *wisdom*. (ST 1211)

It belongs to faith not only that the heart should believe, but also that external words and deeds should bear witness to the inward faith, for confession is an act of faith. (ST 1229)

We are commanded to meditate on the Law in every action of ours, not that we are bound to be always actually thinking about the Law, but that we should regulate all our actions according to it. (ST 1242)

The perfect make progress in charity: yet this is not their chief care, but their aim is principally directed towards union with God ... the beginner, about avoiding sin, with the proficient, about progressing in virtue. (ST 1282)

Among men charity and humility, and not mighty works, are to be esteemed. (CA 290)

Nothing is a greater mark of virtue than to discard superfluities. (CA 376)

To love surpasses being loved, for which reason the greater love is on the part of the benefactor. (ST 1303)

As long as we are in this world, the movement of desire does not cease in us, because it still remains possible for us to approach nearer to God by grace.... When once, however, perfect happiness has been attained, nothing will remain to be desired, because then there will be full enjoyment of God. (ST 1312–13)

The more we think about spiritual goods, the more pleasing they become to us. (ST 1346)

In all the moral virtues, the first mover is prudence, which is called the charioteer of the virtues. (ST 2577)

Prudence is right reason applied to action, just as science is right reason applied to knowledge. (ST 1423)

Seek the fruit of a better life. (ST 2792)

Although one cannot know for certain about another whether he be in the state of salvation, one may infer it with probability from what one sees outwardly of a man: for a tree is known by its fruit (Matt. 7:16). (ST 2846)

The more one will be united to God the happier will one be. Now the measure of charity is the measure of one's union with God. (ST 2971)

A man is said to be wise in respect not of his body but of his soul. (ST 1596)

Christians are sanctified by faith and the sacraments of Christ. (ST 1620)

A man shows himself in life and speech to be what he is. (ST 1671)

Honor is due to virtue, so great honor is due to a great deed of virtue. . . . It savors of excellence that a man is beneficent, generous and grateful. (ST 1731)

It is more perfect to obtain good than to lack evil. Wherefore those virtues like faith, hope, charity, and likewise prudence and justice, which direct one to good simply, are absolutely greater virtues. (ST 1837)

The perfection of charity, in respect of which the Christian life is said to be perfect, consists in our loving God with our whole heart, and our neighbor as ourselves. . . . The love of God and of our neighbor is not commanded according to a measure. (ST 1952)

The perfection of Divine love is a matter of precept for all without exception. (ST 1953)

It is presumptuous to think oneself perfect, but it is not presumptuous to tend to perfection. (ST 1961)

Even as it is better to enlighten than merely to shine, so is it better to give to others the fruits of one's contemplation than merely to contemplate. (ST 1999)

THE
SORROWFUL
MYSTERIES

The First Sorrowful Mystery

The Agony of Jesus in the Garden

Sorrow for Sin

The cares of the world, and the delight in riches, and the desire for other things, enter in and choke the word, and it proves unfruitful.—Mark 4:19

Three things ought chiefly to dissuade us from the sin of pride—firstly, it disorders a man towards God; secondly, towards his neighbors; thirdly, towards himself. (H 27)

Nothing is more foolish than for man, who ought in this present life so to work that he may live eternally, to live idly. . . . From idleness evil is learned, as from a bad master. (H 36–37)

As the blind does not see bodily, so the sinner does not see spiritually. (H 41)

He who despairs of pardon for sin is more bound by his desperation than by the sin which he has committed. Desperation increases despair, and is a greater tyrant than any sin. (H 119)

There are three things which chiefly destroy peace—
(1) pride ... (2) anger ... (3) any kind of iniquity. ...
He who desires in this present life to have peace with
God, with himself, and with his neighbor, and the peace
of eternity for the future, must avoid these three
stumbling-blocks. (H 70)

He who does not bridle his tongue falls into many
sins. ... He who bridles his tongue acquires many good
things. (H 77)

Sin pollutes the mind. ... Great confusion flows from
sin. (H 97)

Repentance consists of three parts. Firstly, of grief of
the heart ... secondly, of confession by the mouth ...
thirdly, in fulfilling the commands of God and the priest.
(H 112)

We should offer our soul to God, being sorry for our
sins: "A sacrifice to God is an afflicted spirit." (C 195)

Only mortal sin excludes us from the kingdom of
God. (C 224)

We must, therefore, make use of things for God's glory
in a way that pleases God and also profits ourselves, so as
to avoid sin in using them. ... Whatever you have, be it

knowledge or beauty, you must refer all and use all for the glory of God. (C 20–21)

Realize that after the angels, man excels all other creatures, and that in no way must we forfeit our dignity on account of sin or for the sake of an inordinate desire for corporeal things which are beneath us and made to serve us. (C 21)

A man thinks that if he sins once he will be able afterward to refrain from sinning, whereas it is quite the reverse that happens. For by the first sin he is weakened and is more inclined to sin again; also sin has a greater power over him. (C 41–42)

If the earth is not cultivated, it brings forth thorns and thistles. In like manner, the sinner's soul, unless it is cultivated by grace, brings forth nothing but the thistles and pricks of sins. (C 121)

The people of this world are wary of evil-doing for fear of temporal punishment. How much more, then, should they be wary for fear of the punishment of Hell, which is greater both in respect to its severity and in respect to its manifold nature: "Remember thy last end, and thou shalt never sin." (C 51)

Whenever you ask for mercy you shall receive it, provided you ask with repentance for your sin.... Every sinner who is contrite and confesses his sin receives mercy. (C 145)

Those who believe more in their own pleasures than in the precepts of God ... worship themselves as gods, for by seeking the pleasures of the flesh, they worship their own bodies instead of God: "Their god is their belly." We must therefore avoid all these things. (C 175)

When we converse with slanderers and laugh with them, when we delight in these frivolities and other faults of the same order, what do we do, if not confirm that evil things do not displease us? (W 11)

In God, there is another perfection, which inclines Him to forgive immediately the gravest and most numerous offenses, if we make a firm resolution to turn from them and truly to amend. Even more, God forgets these offenses in return for a single lamentation of a contrite heart. (W 27)

If it should happen that someone cannot weep, a single word, coming from a contrite heart, suffices for God. It is thus that to the robber who said to Him, "Lord, remember me when Thou shalt come into Thy Kingdom," Jesus replied, "This day thou shalt be with me in Paradise." (W 32)

Knowing that evil is the privation of a due perfection, we can easily understand how evil corrupts good; this it does to the extent that it is the privation of good. Thus blindness is said to corrupt sight because it is the privation of sight. (ss 128)

To say that once a person has sinned he cannot receive the gifts of grace is derogatory to the power of God. Of course, grace cannot coexist with sin; for by grace man is rightly ordered to his end, from which he is turned away by sin. But the contention that sin is irremissible impugns the power of God. (ss 164)

Since by sin man is deflected from his last end, sins cannot be forgiven unless man is again rightly ordered to his end. This is accomplished through the gifts of grace which come from God alone, since they transcend the power of nature. Therefore only God can remit sin. (ss 165)

If there is a definite way of reaching a fixed end, they who travel along a road leading in the opposite direction or who turn aside from the right road, will never reach the goal. A sick man is not cured by using the wrong medicines. . . . Nothing will reach its end unless it performs well the operation proper to it. (ss 197)

Man's extreme unhappiness will consist in the fact that his intellect is completely shut off from the divine light, and that his affections are stubbornly turned against God's goodness. And this is the chief suffering of the damned. It is known as the punishment of loss. (ss 199)

If God had decided to restore man solely by an act of His will and power, the order of divine justice would not have been observed. Justice demands satisfaction for sin. (SS 229)

The more anyone is detached from the things of the flesh, the more he is filled with spiritual goods. For man is raised up by spiritual goods but dragged down by carnal attractions. (SS 274–75)

Sin is committed by cleaving to changeable goods in contempt of the changeless Good. (SS 323)

Since evil is opposed to good, the presence of all good requires the utter banishment of evil. Justice has no participation with injustice, and light has no fellowship with darkness. (SS 363)

Things get more deficient not by getting closer to something altogether deficient, but by getting further away from something perfect; for this is what lack and deficiency mean . . . which is why we find big mistakes grow from small beginnings. (SP 159)

Unless one resists habit it compels one. (SP 175)

God is said to give people up to foul desires or to bend their wills to evil not by acting on them and moving them, but by deserting them and not interfering. . . . But God's judgement that he will not help some who fall is just. (SP 292)

Sins aren't caused by our aggressive or affective tendencies as God set them up in us, but by disorders in those tendencies. He set them up to obey reason, and any tendency to sin, against reason, is not from God. (SP 293)

Sin's evilness isn't in any way included in God's will, but is a consequence of our free choice abandoning its relationship to God's will. (SP 296)

Mistakes of reason and conscience, then, made willingly, whether directly willed or arising from neglect of what it is our duty to know, do not excuse a will consenting to mistaken reason and conscience from acting badly. . . . The mistake comes from not knowing a law of God which it was his duty to know. (SP 371)

An action's consequences can be foreseen or unforseen. . . . Not to refrain from an action even when one sees it could have many bad consequences shows a deeper disorder in the will. (SP 388)

In God, we may consider both His justice, in respect of which He punishes those who sin, and His mercy, in respect of which He sets us free: in us the consideration of His justice gives rise to fear, but the consideration of His mercy gives rise to hope. (ST 1250)

If a man turn to God and adhere to Him, through fear of punishment, it will be servile fear; but if it be on account of fear of committing a fault, it will be filial fear, for it becomes a child to fear offending its father. (ST 1251)

As it is false that God does not pardon the repentant, or that He does not turn sinners to repentance, so is it false that He grants forgiveness to those who persevere in their sins, and that He gives glory to those who cease from good works. (ST 1263)

To sin with the intention of persevering in sin and through the hope of being pardoned, is presumptuous, and this does not diminish, but increases sin. (ST 1263)

Venial sin is a disorder about things directed to the end. . . . Thus sick people sometimes, though they love health much, are irregular in keeping to their diet. (ST 1283)

Why do you oppose your own salvation? (CA 451)

All should avoid the society of sinners, as regards fellowship in sin. (ST 1290)

Man is in one sense without life, who is without Him who said, *I am the life.* (CA 664)

The good man when taken in a sin has sorrow because he has sinned, the bad man is grieved not because he has sinned, but because he is found out in his sin; and he not only does not repent, but is indignant with him that reproved him. (CA 736)

While men would avoid present punishment, they overlook that which is to come. (CA 770)

As the body, when the spirit departs, first becomes cold, and then decays and decomposes; so also your temple, when God's Spirit shall have withdrawn, shall first be filled with strife and anarchy, and after shall come to ruin. (CA 797)

No man stumbles spiritually, without being kept back somewhat from advancing in God's way, and that is at least a venial sin. (ST 1368)

Contrition is *humility of the soul.* (ST 2574)

The time for contrition is the whole of the present state of life. For as long as one is a wayfarer, one detests the obstacles which retard or hinder one from reaching the end of the way. (ST 2583)

Inordinate love is its own punishment, as Augustine states. (ST 3002)

Works of virtue belong especially to the state of happiness, and their contraries to the state of unhappiness. (ST 3005)

It is clear that it is wrong to remain in sin even for a short time; and one is bound to renounce one's sin at once, according to Sirach 21:2, *Flee from sin as from the face of a serpent.* (ST 1462)

It is unlawful to co-operate in an evil deed, by counseling, helping, or in any way consenting, because to counsel or assist in an action is, in a way, to do it. (ST 1498–99)

There is nothing to hinder mortal sin from arising out of venial sin, since venial sin is a disposition to mortal. (ST 1647)

He that helps another to commit a sin does him not a favor but an injury. (ST 1653)

Man is able by himself to fall into sin, but he cannot by himself arise from sin without the help of grace. (ST 1756)

It belongs to the virtuous man to avoid not only vice, but also whatever has the semblance of vice, according to 1 Thessalonians 5:22, *From all appearance of evil refrain yourselves.* (ST 1780)

Lust applies chiefly to venereal pleasures, which more than anything else work the greatest havoc in a man's mind. . . . By inordinately using the body through lust a man wrongs God Who is the Supreme Lord of our body. (ST 1810 and 1812)

In very truth some sadness is praiseworthy, . . . namely, when it flows from holy love, as, for instance, when a man is saddened over his own or others' sins. Furthermore, it is employed as a useful means of satisfying for sins. (ST 2271)

We must take note that every sin committed directly against human life is a mortal sin. (ST 1816)

Concupiscence is fain to disguise itself and creeps in by stealth. (ST 1834)

When a man passes from sin to grace, he passes from servitude to freedom. . . . Charity causes the change of condition from spiritual servitude to spiritual freedom. (ST 1954)

The Devil does not straight away tempt the spiritual man to grave sins, but he begins with lighter sins, so as gradually to lead him to those of greater magnitude. (ST 2244)

It is a sin to desire worldly riches and honor in an inordinate fashion. And the principal sign of this is when a man does something wrong in order to acquire such things. (ST 2244)

It belongs to penance to detest one's past sins, and to purpose, at the same time, to change one's life for the better, which is the end, so to speak, of penance. (ST 2565)

Since the wretchedness to which vice leads is opposed to the happiness to which virtue leads, whatever pertains to wretchedness must be understood as being the opposite of all we have said about happiness. (SS 199)

The Second Sorrowful Mystery

The Scourging at the Pillar

Purity

Clean the inside of cup and dish first so that the outside may become clean as well.—Matthew 23:26

There are three things which the Lord requires of His servants—the first, that they should be cleansed from every defilement of sin; the second, that they should be ornamented with every virtue; the third, that they should be decorated with honesty of manners. (H 11)

Purity, humility, and justice prepare the way of the Lord. (H 16)

Justice regulates us in regard to our neighbors, and Purity with regard to ourselves. (H 17)

Interior perfection consists in—*firstly*, a knowledge of the truth; and *secondly*, the delight in goodness. The first of these implies the perfection of the understanding, the second the perfection of the affections. (H 176–77)

Morally, if anyone desires to attain unto the glory of eternity, he must study to be a child—to be pure in three things. *Firstly*, in the heart . . . *secondly*, in the mouth . . . *thirdly*, in deed. (H 179)

We are encouraged to keep our souls pure, because our nature was ennobled and raised through being united to God, to the extent of being assumed into union with a divine Person. (C 36)

When a man sins, he defiles his soul. Just as virtue is the soul's beauty, so is sin its stain. (C 40)

The Holy Spirit cleanses us from our sins. This is because a thing is repaired by the same one who made it. Now, the soul is created by the Holy Spirit because by Him God makes all things, for it is through loving His own goodness that God is the cause of all. (C 73–74)

If men lead a pure life they are saved. (C 87)

When we do not consent to temptation, we keep our hearts clean, of which it is said: "Blessed are the clean of heart, for they shall see God." (C 154)

The good physician removes the external symptoms of a malady. Furthermore, he even removes the very root of the illness so that there will be no relapse. So, also, the Lord wishes us to avoid the beginnings of sins. (C 219)

In God there is another perfection, which is that He does not judge human acts on their exterior appearance; but He discerns all, in His immense and ineffable wisdom, according to the intentions of the heart. (W 45)

The more our intention is pure and strongly directed toward God, the less we dwell upon our own advantages and even upon those of other men, and the more our works will be agreeable to God and profitable to all. (W 66–67)

Give to me a noble heart, which no unworthy desire can debase. Give to me a resolute heart, which no evil intention can divert. Give to me a stalwart heart, which no tribulation can overcome. Give to me a temperate heart, which no violent passion can enslave. (P 11)

He did well to extol purity of life at His very birth, by being born of a virgin. (SS 275)

The Son of God assumed flesh and came into the world to raise us to resurrection, in which men "shall neither marry nor be married, but shall be as the angels of God in Heaven." This is why He inculcated the doctrine of continence and of virginal integrity, that an image of the glory that is to come might, in some degree, shine forth in the lives of the faithful. (SS 275)

The atmosphere is not beautiful save when it is transfigured by sunlight, and the soul is not perfect except it be subject to God. In this, then, consists our blessedness, that we be subject to God. (T 17)

In order that we may see God clearly, we must have eyes undimmed. If our eyes are misty or turbid, they are unable to see the brightness of the sun. Similarly if in your soul there is the fire of concupiscence, the fire of anger, or the fire of evil desires, you are hindered from the vision of God. (T 19)

God on his side gives to everything as much of himself as it can take in; and if something falls short of its share in God's goodness, that must be because it presents some obstacle to the sharing ... by the recipient, who turns away from a light that never turns itself away. (SP 293)

Virtue itself must be a sort of ordered condition of soul in which the soul's powers are ordered among themselves and to the outside world. Virtue then is a sort of fitness of soul and can be likened to health and beauty, which are right conditions of the body. (SP 394)

The peacemakers are pronounced blessed, they namely who make peace first within their own hearts, then between brethren at variance. For what avails it to make peace between others, while in your own heart are wars of rebellious vices. (CA 154)

Nothing is more innocent than he who is sound and of perfect health in virtue. (CA 198)

The first beginning of the heart's purifying is faith; and if this be perfected through being quickened by charity, the heart will be perfectly purified. (ST 1203)

Truth and falsehood in the intellect correspond to good and evil in the appetite. (ST 1259)

No sin can grow from a virtuous root. (ST 1260)

The fact that spiritual goods taste good to us no more, or seem to be goods of no great account, is chiefly due to our affections being infected with the love of bodily pleasures, among which, sexual pleasures hold the first place: for the love of those pleasures leads man to have a distaste for spiritual things. (ST 1262)

Not every friendship is praiseworthy and virtuous, as in the case of friendship based on pleasure or utility. (ST 1271)

For us to love God above all things in this way, it is necessary that charity be infused into our hearts. . . . Charity proceeds from *a pure heart, and a good conscience, and an unfeigned faith*. (ST 1276)

As in the eyes of man a fair face has grace, so in the eyes of God a pure conscience has favor. (CA 241)

One's conscience should be preferred to a good name. (ST 1339)

Vice is contrary to man's nature, in as much as he is a rational animal: and when a thing acts contrary to its nature, that which is natural to it is corrupted little by little. (ST 1343)

Who can discern a treasure buried in the ground, or the sun when obscured by a cloud? (CA 673)

In the sense that a man's whole heart be habitually directed to God, so that it consent to nothing contrary to the love of God, ... this is the perfection of the way. (ST 1376)

Virginity of the mind can be restored, although virginity of the flesh cannot. (ST 2987)

Virginity is said to be an angelic life, in so far as virgins imitate by grace what angels have by nature. (ST 2993)

A secure and calm conscience is a great good, according to Proverbs 15:15, *A secure mind is like a continual feast.* (ST 1509)

All are obliged to offer to God a devout mind. (ST 1557)

Since kindness depends on the heart rather than on the deed, so too gratitude depends chiefly on the heart.

(ST 1651)

Although beauty is becoming to every virtue, it is ascribed to temperance, ... which consists in a certain moderate and fitting proportion, and this is what we understand by beauty. (ST 1766)

The beauty of the body consists in a man having his bodily limbs well proportioned, together with a certain clarity of color. In like manner spiritual beauty consists in a man's conduct or actions being well proportioned in respect of the spiritual clarity of reason. Now this is what is meant by honesty.... Honesty is the same as spiritual beauty. (ST 1781–82)

It is true that purity, as to its essence, is in the soul; but as to its matter, it is in the body: and it is the same with virginity.... It is a spiritual thing, which a holy continency fosters and preserves. (ST 1806)

Surpassing beauty is ascribed to chastity.... Virgins *follow the Lamb whithersoever He goeth*, because they imitate Christ, by integrity not only of the mind but also of the flesh. (ST 1810)

Modesty regards not only outward but also inward actions. (ST 1847)

Moderation of the inner man may be shown by certain outward signs.... The inner man precedes the outward man. (ST 1847 and 1853)

Women are not forbidden to adorn themselves soberly and moderately but to do so excessively, shamelessly, and immodestly. (ST 1883)

To keep oneself innocent in face of a greater peril is proof of greater virtue. (ST 1959)

What is of God is well-ordered. (ST 2211)

Souls become good and just by sharing in the Divine goodness. . . . The soul is beatified by a participation with God. (ST 2326)

God's wisdom will separate the pure from the impure. He will gather up only the wheat in His barns, . . . that is to say, He will reward in Heaven and will allow to serve for the good of all only that which has, with a pure intention, been done, or omitted, or suffered for Him alone. (W 67)

THE THIRD SORROWFUL MYSTERY

THE CROWNING WITH THORNS

Courage

Courage! It is I! Do not be afraid.
—Matthew 14:27

"Let us put on the armor of light." For the arms of light are mercy and truth; for mercy is the shield by which we are defended from the enemy, and truth is the power by which we overcome all things. (H 4)

We ought by holiness to war against the demons. (H 31)

Fortitude or strength becomes the strength of hope in a holy soul. (H 182)

Those who are reborn in the spirit need to be fortified by the Holy Spirit. Hence the Apostles, in order to become strong, received the Holy Spirit after Christ's Ascension: "Stay you in the city till you be endowed with power from on high." (C 85)

Break off all delays, rise from sleep, and do that which is commanded. (CA 57)

A man's virtue is tried sometimes as regards his doing good, sometimes as regards his avoiding evil.... If he offers strong resistance and does not consent, his virtue is great. (C 150)

He who does not speak the truth freely also betrays it, for it must be freely spoken; also he who does not defend it boldly, betrays it, for it must be boldly defended. (W 50)

By His death Christ also gave an example of *fortitude*, which does not abandon justice in the face of adversity. Refusal to give up the practice of virtue even under fear of death seems to pertain most emphatically to fortitude.

(SS 290)

Clearly charity is not only a virtue, but the most potent of all virtues. (SP 424)

In the end we must take our departure from the stage of this world, and there remains that the reward of resurrection and glory follow the victory over temptation.

(CA 8)

When God's honor and our neighbor's good demand, man should not be contented with being united by faith to God's truth, but ought to confess his faith outwardly.

(ST 1189)

Firmness and strength of walking by the way of wisdom in good habits is thus set before us, by which men are brought to purity and simplicity of heart. (CA 276)

As the Church built by Christ cannot be thrown down, so any such Christian who has built himself upon Christ, no adversity can overthrow, according to that, *Who shall separate us from the love of Christ?* (CA 292)

What is brought on by prosperity is broken off by adversity. None of these things does he fear who has his house founded upon a rock, that is, who not only hears the command of the Lord, but who also does it. (CA 293)

Nothing ought to be more binding on us than the business of heaven.... To this we ought to apply ourselves with all our endeavors, and not to be slack, however necessary or urgent are the things that draw us aside. (CA 318)

In what measure we have borne witness to Him upon earth, in the same shall we have Him to bear witness to us in heaven before the face of God the Father. (CA 393)

The good ground is the faithful conscience of the elect, or the spirit of the saints which receives the word of God with joy and desire and devotion of heart, and manfully retains it amid prosperous and adverse circumstances, and brings it forth in fruit. (CA 492)

When our own means fail, then those which are of God stand. (CA 542)

Our love for God is proved to be so much the stronger, as the more difficult are the things we accomplish for its sake. (ST 1310)

The general in a battle loves best that soldier who turns in this flight and courageously presses the enemy, than him who never turned his back, yet never did any valorous deed. (CA 631)

Admire Christ's power, and the courage of the disciples. . . . The Romans conquered countless thousands of Jews, but could not overcome twelve unarmed unprotected men. (CA 811)

He that thinks he knows somewhat, when he knows nothing, is an easy conquest for one who has understanding. Thus the attacks of an enemy are vehement at first, but if one endure them with a courageous spirit, he will find them more feeble. (CA 759)

What might is the power of the cross. Adam set at nought the commandment, taking the apple from the tree; but all Adam lost, Christ found upon the cross.

(CA 950)

It would not be right to avoid scandal so as to desert justice: for the truth should not be gainsayed for fear of scandal. Wherefore when justice and truth are in the balance, a man should not be deterred by the fear of giving scandal. (ST 2611)

The Christian religion prevailed. (ST 2811)

The most perfect and most brilliant kind of victory is never to have yielded to the foe: and the crown is due, not to the battle but to the victory gained by the battle.

(ST 2987)

We merit only through that which is in us. And the more that which one suffers voluntarily is difficult and naturally repugnant to the will, the more is the will that suffers it for Christ's sake shown to be firmly established in Christ. (ST 2990)

Participate in the perfect victory by imitating Him in Whom the fulness of perfect victory is realized.... Since in Christ the notion of victory is found chiefly and fully, for by His victory other[s] are made victors. (ST 2992)

The martyr's battle is more strenuous in itself, and more intensely painful; while the conflict with the flesh is fraught with greater danger, inasmuch as it is more lasting and threatens us at closer quarters. (ST 2995)

It helps to resist the assaults of all vices. For he that can stand firm in things that are most difficult to bear, is prepared, in consequence, to resist those which are less difficult. (ST 1708)

Fortitude of soul must be that which binds the will firmly to the good of reason in face of the greatest evils: because he that stands firm against great things, will in consequence stand firm against less things, but not conversely. (ST 1709)

Combine execution with greatness of purpose. . . . Without them there can be no fortitude. (ST 1726)

The act of fortitude consists not only in holding fast to good against the fear of future dangers, but also in not failing through sorrow or pain occasioned by things present. (ST 1752)

It belongs to perseverance to persevere to the end of the virtuous work, for instance that a soldier persevere to the end of the fight, and the magnificent man until his work be accomplished. There are, however, some virtues whose acts must endure throughout the whole of life, such as faith, hope, and charity, since they regard the last end of the entire life of man. (ST 1754)

Our Lord declared that it belongs to the perfection of life that a man follow Him, not anyhow, but in such a way as not to turn back. (ST 1977)

The help of the Holy Ghost, who is the Author of the perfect deed, is more powerful than the assault of the envious Devil. (ST 2242)

A soldier cannot conquer unless he obey his captain. And so the Man–Christ secured the victory through being obedient to God, according to Proverbs 21:28: *An obedient man shall speak of victory.* (ST 2279)

There is always a remedy provided through Christ's Passion. (ST 2289)

The Holy Ghost is given to the baptized for strength: just as He was given to the apostles on the day of Pentecost. . . . The Holy Ghost is not sent or given except with sanctifying grace. (ST 2429)

Sanctifying grace does indeed take away sin; but it has other effects also, because it suffices to carry man through every step as far as eternal life. (ST 2429)

A man's triumph over another is complete when he conquers him not only in the open field, but attacks him in his stronghold and deprives him of his kingdom and even of his dwelling place. Now, Christ had triumphed over the devil and had conquered him on the Cross. (C 48)

Grant to me, O Lord my God, that I may not falter in times of prosperity or adversity, so that I may not be exalted in the former, nor dejected in the latter. (P 5 and 7)

The longer love lasts, the stronger it is. (ST 1301)

The Holy Ghost works this in man, by bringing him to everlasting life, which is the end of all good deeds, and the release from all perils. A certain confidence of this is infused into the mind by the Holy Ghost Who expels any fear of the contrary. It is in this sense that fortitude is reckoned a gift of the Holy Ghost. (ST 1759)

This gift of fortitude prevents man's heart from fainting through fear of lacking necessities, and makes him trust without wavering that God will provide him with whatever he needs. For this reason the Holy Spirit, the giver of fortitude, teaches us to pray to God to *give us this day our daily bread.* (C 137)

THE FOURTH SORROWFUL MYSTERY

THE CARRYING OF THE CROSS

Patience

As for [the seeds] in the good soil, they are those who, hearing the word, hold it fast in an honest and good heart, and bring forth fruit with patience.—Luke 8:15

We must run perseveringly, so that we forsake not the course, nor fail of well-doing—(Matt. 24:13), "He that shall endure unto the end, the same shall be saved." (H 35)

Patience is chiefly needed to enable us to persevere, and to bear all the troubles which come upon us in this world. (H 35)

If endured in love eternal blessedness is the fruit of labor. (H 38)

That which is the length of charity is the length of perseverance. . . . This is that which lifts the soul on high, that God may be expected for a reward. (H 122)

It is easy, indeed, to place a veil before the eyes, and to wear poor clothing, and to walk with the head bowed down; but patient endurance of wrong proves who is truly humble. (H 128)

We ought to persevere in good.... For the reward is earned by perseverance alone. (H 123)

After death the day of man is ended and the day of Christ begins.... Persevere in this course till the day of Christ. (H 143)

Pressed down under so many labors we need to come to Christ, Who refreshes us with a threefold food. (1) With the "Bread of Life" ... this is the reception of the Body of Christ. (2) With the hidden manna ... this is the sweetness of spiritual devotion. (3) With the tree of life ... this is to partake of the fruits of the Spirit. (H 171)

No evil comes from God except insofar as it is directed to a good. Consequently, if all the pains a man suffers come from God, he must bear them patiently. For by pain sins are cleansed, the guilty are humbled, and the good are urged on to the love of God. (C 20)

If you seek an example of patience, you will find a most perfect example on the Cross. For a man's patience is proved to be great on two counts: either when he suffers great evils patiently or when he suffers that which he is able to avoid yet does not avoid. (C 44)

If man overcomes temptation he deserves a crown.... Again: "Blessed is the man that is patient under temptation, for when he hath been proved he shall receive the crown of life." (C 153)

He delivers us from afflictions when He comforts us in them. For unless He comforts us, we cannot endure. . . . "According to the multitude of my sorrows in my heart, Thy comforts delight my soul." (C 156)

He delivers us from evil insofar as temptations and trials are conductive to our profit. Thus He does not say, *Deliver us from trials*, but *from evil*, because trials bring the saints a crown, and for that reason they glory in their trials. (C 156)

By patience we obtain peace whether times be good or evil. For this reason, peacemakers are called the children of God because they are like God: just as nothing can hurt God, so nothing can harm them, whether they prosper or suffer. (C 157)

[Our Lord's] patience in His Passion is shown in three ways—(1) in that He voluntarily offered Himself . . . (2) because, unjustly judged, He endure it with the greatest patience . . . (3) because He did not utter threats against His crucifiers. (H 70–71)

Final happiness, which is reached by virtuous action, is a good that belongs not to this life but to the next life. (SS 198)

[Christ] gave an example of *patience*, a virtue that prevents sorrow from overwhelming man in time of adversity. The greater the trials, the more splendidly does the virtue of patience shine forth in them. (SS 291)

First He corrects a man, then He schools him, and finally takes him up to Himself. That God's correction is the way to blessedness follow from Job: *Blessed is the man whom God correcteth.* This correction is a part of God's call. (T 2)

If a man would come to some exalted state, he must ascend by little and little. (T 7)

It is no small sign of goodness to bear poverty easily, to live by honest labor, and to be bound together by virtue of affection. (CA 138)

Man in sorrow receives great comfort from the recollection of the sufferings of others, who are set before him as an example of patience. (CA 159)

There is no example of patience more perfect than that of the Lord. (CA 198)

The Christian mind is most patient, and prepared to endure. (CA 201)

A man hopes to obtain eternal life, not by his own power (since this would be an act of presumption), but with the help of grace; and if he perseveres therein he will obtain eternal life surely and infallibly. (ST 1171)

We are called wayfarers by reason of our being on the way to God, Who is the last end of our happiness. (ST 1277)

One act of charity makes man more ready to act again according to charity, and this readiness increasing, man breaks out into an act of more fervent love, and strives to advance in charity.... Yet this increase does not take place at once, but when we strive for that increase. (ST 1279–80)

In Scripture, charity is compared to fire.... Now fire ever mounts upward so long as it lasts. Therefore as long as charity endures, it can ascend, but cannot descend. (ST 1282)

To pass through toil and sweat, and to arrive at a good end, namely life, is sufficient solace to those who undergo these struggles. For if sailors can make light of storms and soldiers of wounds in hope of perishable rewards, much more when Heaven lies before, and rewards immortal, will none look to the impending dangers. (CA 279–80)

The reward is not for those that begin, but those that bring to an end.... To endure in Christ, is to abide in His faith. (CA 384)

We are to abide in patience until the harvest-time. (CA 498)

In this present Church there cannot be bad without good, nor good without bad. He is not good who refuses to endure the bad. (CA 746)

Tribulation gives hope of salvation, by making us exercise our own virtue. (ST 2606)

God causes in us virtue and knowledge, not only when we first acquire them, but also as long as we persevere in them: and it is thus that God causes in the blessed a knowledge of what is to be done. (ST 1414)

The crown is due to one who has striven. (ST 2989)

Just as we need patience in things done against us, so do we need it in those said against us. (ST 1502)

Now it belongs to fortitude of the mind to bear bravely with infirmities of the flesh, and this belongs to the virtue of patience or fortitude, so also to acknowledge one's infirmity, and this belongs to the perfection that is called humility. (ST 1707)

God's grace ... has more strength to raise the soul to the Divine things in which it delights, than bodily pains have to afflict it. (ST 1712)

Strength of will is the same as patience or forebearance. (ST 1727)

The act of patience, in heaven, will not consist in bearing things, but in enjoying the goods to which we had aspired by suffering.... That which we shall obtain by patience will be eternal. (ST 1750)

Patience safeguards the mind from being overcome by sorrow. (ST 1750)

Possession denotes undisturbed ownership; wherefore man is said to possess his soul by patience, in so far as it removes by the root the passions that are evoked by hardships and disturb the soul. (ST 1751)

Fortitude denotes a certain firmness of mind. . . . This firmness of mind is required both in doing good and in enduring evil, especially with regard to goods or evils that are difficult. (ST 1758–59)

Patience is stated to have a perfect work in relation to charity, in so far as it is an effect of the abundance of charity that a man bears hardships patiently. (ST 1951)

It is evident that no one comes to the summit suddenly, since every man that lives aright, progresses during the whole course of his life, so as to arrive at the summit. (ST 2006)

Magnificence consists not only in being constant in the accomplishment of great deeds, which belongs to constancy, but also in bringing a certain manly prudence and solicitude to that accomplishment. (ST 1727)

The Fifth Sorrowful Mystery

The Crucifixion

Self-Denial

If any man would come after me, let him deny himself and take up his cross daily and follow me.—Luke 9:23

A fourfold profit flows from fasting—(1) The mortification of vices. (2) An elevation of the mind towards God. (3) The acquisition of virtue. (4) The reward of eternal blessedness. (H 47–48)

Whosoever desires to follow Christ ought entirely to surrender his life. (H 68)

What need was there for the Word of God to suffer for us? That the need was great may be assigned to two reasons. One was the need for a remedy for sin; the other was the need for an example of what we ought to do. (C 40)

The more a man conforms to the Passion of Christ, the more is he pardoned and the more grace he merits. (C 43)

Christ's Passion [is] a model of virtues. Accordingly it is clear how profitable was Christ's Passion as a remedy, but it is not less profitable as an example.... There is no virtue an example of which we do not find on the Cross. (C 43–44)

If you seek an example of charity, "greater love hath no man than that he lays down his life for his friends," and this Christ did on the Cross. If He laid down His life for us, we should not deem it a hardship to suffer any evils whatever for His sake. (C 44)

Between the spirit and the flesh there is a continual combat. Now, if you wish the spirit to win, you must assist it by prayer and resist the flesh by such means as fasting (for by fasting the flesh is weakened). (C 248)

From him for whom He has remitted a greater number of sins, or graver sins, and from him whom He has preserved from them, He awaits a more generous love and more worthy fruits of penitence. (W 41)

Another reason why He wished to die was that His death might be for us not only a remedy of satisfaction but also a sacrament of salvation, so that we, transferred to a spiritual life, might die to our carnal life, in the likeness of His death. (SS 290)

Christ also wished to die that His death might be an example of perfect virtue for us. He gave an example of

charity. . . . The more numerous and grievous are the sufferings a person does not refuse to bear for his friend,
the more strikingly his love is shown forth. (SS 290)

Whatever is within you is subject to your nature, but
that which makes you blessed ought to be above you,
not subject to you. (T 18)

Natural reason leads us to offer sensible things to God
as a sign of the subjection and honor we owe him, rather
as we offer things to our temporal masters in recogni-
tion of their authority. This is what we call *sacrifice*, so
offering sacrifice is an act of natural justice. (SP xxv)

When we fast for God's sake, the fasting acquires a goodness from being done for God. (SP 373)

Let Thy will be done as in Heaven, so in earth; that is, as the
spirit does not resist God, so let the body not resist the
spirit. (CA 227)

If you cast out all wickedness from your heart, you have
washed your conscience, and fast well. Fasting ought to
be fulfilled not in abstinence of food only, but much
more in cutting off vices. (CA 241)

If a man can control the greatest pleasures, much more
can he control lesser ones. (ST 1768)

Unless a man departs from himself, he does not draw near to Him who is above him. . . . It is therefore then that we leave and deny ourselves, when we avoid that which we were of old, and strive towards that to which we are called. (CA 593)

He who prays with his fasting has two wings, lighter than the winds themselves. . . . His zeal is as the warmth of fire, and his constancy as the firmness of the earth. (CA 615)

After the discourse in which the Lord had declared that He should return in splendor, He announced to the Apostles His approaching Passion, that they might learn the close connection between the sacrament of the Cross, and the glory of eternity. (CA 873)

We have but three kinds of goods, bodily, spiritual, and goods of fortune, or external goods. By almsdeeds we deprive ourselves of some goods of fortune, and by fasting we retrench goods of the body. As to goods of the soul, there is no need to deprive ourselves of any of them. (ST 2623)

Every sin is committed either against God, and this is prevented by *prayer*, or against our neighbor, and this is remedied by *almsdeeds*, or against ourselves, and this is forestalled by *fasting*. (ST 2623)

Where a man is accustomed to enjoy pleasures, it is more difficult for him to endure the lack of them. . . .

His mind is less persevering through the frailty of his temperament. (ST 1757)

Man naturally desires pleasures that are becoming to him. Since, however, man as such is a rational being, it follows that those pleasures are becoming to man which are in accordance with reason. From such pleasures temperance does not withdraw him, but from those which are contrary to reason. (ST 1765)

The gift of fear has as its principal object God, Whom it avoids offending.... Man stands in the greatest need of the fear of God in order to shun those things which are most seductive, and these are the matter of temperance.

(ST 1765)

The end and rule of temperance itself is happiness.

(ST 1769)

The very fact that the reason is able to moderate desires and pleasures that are furthest removed from it, proves the greatness of reason's power. This is how temperance comes to be a principal virtue. (ST 1770)

Athletes and soldiers have to deny themselves many pleasures, in order to fulfil their respective duties. In like manner penitents, in order to recover health of soul, have recourse to abstinence from pleasures, as a kind of diet, and those who are desirous of giving themselves up to contemplation and Divine things need much to refrain from carnal things. (ST 1772)

In abstaining from food a man should act with due regard
for those among whom he lives, for his own person, and
for the requirements of health. (ST 1784)

Right reason makes one abstain as one ought, i.e. with
gladness of heart, and for the due end, i.e. for God's
glory and not one's own. (ST 1784)

Properly speaking fasting consists in abstaining from food,
but speaking metaphorically it denotes abstinence from
anything harmful, and such especially is sin. (ST 1786)

Fasting is useful as atoning for and preventing sin, and
as raising the mind to spiritual things. And everyone is
bound by the natural dictate of reason to practice fasting
as far as it is necessary for these purposes. (ST 1787)

Fasting considered in itself is commendable at all times;
thus Jerome wrote: *Would that we might fast always*. (ST 1790)

All the things that belong properly to temperance are
necessary to the present life, and their excess is harmful.
Wherefore it behooves one to apply a measure in all such
things. (ST 1797)

Chastity takes its name from the fact that reason *chas-
tises* concupiscence, which, like a child, needs curb-

ing. . . . The essence of human virtue consists in being something moderated by reason. (ST 1802)

Virtue can be recovered by penance. (ST 1808)

The good of reason flourishes more in the temperate man. (ST 1830)

No price is worthy of a continent soul, because its value is not measured with gold or silver. (ST 1830)

Austerity, as a virtue, does not exclude all pleasures, but only such as are excessive and inordinate. (ST 1881)

It is clear that fasting, watching, obedience, and the like withdraw man from sins of gluttony and lust and all other manner of sins. (ST 2005)

The love of God to men is shown not merely in the assumption of human nature, but especially in what He suffered in human nature for other men. (ST 2055)

A penitent can give a praiseworthy example, not by having sinned, but by freely bearing the punishment of sin. And hence Christ set the highest example to penitents, since He willingly bore the punishment, not of His own sin, but of the sins of others. (ST 2106)

"If any man will come after Me" (Lk. 9:23) . . . He who so dies will come to that life in which no one dies; to which life may Christ, Who is our life, bring us. (H 68)

It was becoming that Christ should wish to fast before His temptation. First, in order to give us an example. For since we are all in urgent need of strengthening our-selves against temptation, . . . He teaches us the need of fasting in order to equip ourselves against temptation.

(ST 2242)

There was the spiritual fire of charity in Christ's holocaust. (ST 2269)

This kind of death was especially suitable in order to atone for the sin of our first parent, which was the pluck-ing of the apple from the forbidden tree against God's command. And so, to atone for that sin, it was fitting that Christ should suffer by being fastened to a tree, as if restoring what Adam had purloined. (ST 2268)

It is indeed a wicked and cruel act to hand over an inno-cent man to torment and to death against his will. Yet God the Father did not so deliver up Christ, but inspired Him with the will to suffer for us. (ST 2280)

THE
GLORIOUS
MYSTERIES

THE FIRST GLORIOUS MYSTERY

THE RESURRECTION OF JESUS
FROM THE DEAD

Faith

Blessed are those who have not seen and yet believe.
—John 20:29

He served us by redeeming us. . . . He will further preserve us to glory. (H 11)

He who is of God has everything which is best. (H 58)

Jesus is interpreted Savior, since He wished to die that He might save by His death, and show His infinite goodness. . . . The death of Christ was such an inestimable love of charity as no mere man was able to conceive of.
(H 66)

There are three reasons why Christ is called the "Good Shepherd," since His office is threefold—(1) to defend the sheep; (2) to lead and feed them in good pastures; and (3) to restore those who are wandering. (H 72)

This Name of Jesus is ever to be invoked, since it both justifies sinners and saves the elect. (H 180)

Place Christ, Who is our rock, in the nest of the heart "That Christ may dwell in your hearts by faith" (Eph. 3:17). (H 160)

The first thing a Christian needs is faith, without which no man is a faithful Christian. . . . Faith unites the soul to God, because by faith the Christian soul is in a sense wedded to God. (C 5)

Faith introduces eternal life into us, for eternal life is nothing else than to know God. Thus our Lord said, "This is eternal life, to know Thee, the only true God." This knowledge of God begins in us by faith, and is perfected in the life to come, when we shall know Him as He is. (C 6)

Faith is our guide in the present life, since in order to lead a good life a man needs to know what is necessary to live rightly. (C 6)

If we were able by ourselves to know perfectly all things, visible and invisible, it would be foolish for us to believe what we do not see. But our knowledge is so imperfect that no philosopher has ever been able to discover perfectly the nature of a single fly. . . . If our intelligence is so weak, is it not foolish to be willing to believe about God only what we are able to find out by ourselves alone? (C 8)

We should believe what is of faith even more than the things that we see, since man's sight may be deceived, whereas God's knowledge is never at fault. (C 10)

God governs all things. It will do well to consider what is meant by this word *God*, for it signifies the governor and provider of all things. To believe there is a God is to believe in one whose government and Providence extend to all things. (C 10)

The maker is greater than the things he makes. Since God is the Maker of all things, it follows that He is greater than all things. (C 19)

Not only must Christians believe in one God, and that He is the Creator of Heaven and earth and of all things, but they must also believe that God is the Father, of whom Christ is the true Son. (C 23)

If anyone were to tell us about a distant country which he had never visited, we would not believe him to the same extent as if he had been there ... believe Christ, who was with God, who indeed was one with God. For this reason our faith is very strong, seeing that we have received it from Christ. (C 35)

That Christ did indeed die for us is so hard to conceive that scarcely is our mind able to grasp it.... So great is God's favor and love in our regard that He has done more for us than we are able to understand. (C 39)

Although He died, it was neither through weakness nor of necessity, but through power, since He chose to die. This is evident from the fact that in the moment of dying He cried out with a loud voice, which others cannot do at the moment of death, for they die from weakness. For this reason, the centurion exclaimed, "Verily this was the Son of God." (C 54)

The Word of God is the Son of God, just as man's word is a concept of man's intellect. Now, man's word is sometimes a dead word; for instance, if he thinks of what he ought to do, but does not have the will to do it. Such is faith without works, in which case faith is said to be dead. (C 71)

Evil cannot destroy the glory of God.... For the evil with which He punishes and the good with which He rewards redound to God's glory. (C 160)

He has considered, uniquely, the abundance of His eternal and immense goodness, and ordered all for the greatest good of the angelic and the human creation. In creating and preserving the heavens, the four elements, and all that they enclose, God does not consider His own interest, but rather what is advantageous for men and angels. (W 65)

All that God does today . . . whether the air be cold or warm; whether it rain or blow; whether the road be dry or humid; whether the fruits of the earth abound or perish—it is impossible that all this could be better at any given moment, because the immense wisdom of God by an extreme charity and benignity produces each thing at the very time it is needed. (w 70)

If God is infinite in His essence, His power must be infinite. (ss 22)

Higher rulers personally take charge of great concerns, and entrust the management of unimportant affairs to others. But God can take cognizance of a multitude of things simultaneously. . . . Hence the fact that He attends to the slightest details does not keep Him from organizing the weightiest matters. (ss 148)

Immaterial substances cannot be made from preexisting matter. Consequently they can be produced only by God through creation. For this reason the Catholic Faith professes that God is the "Creator of Heaven and Earth, and of all things visible," and also "of all things invisible." (ss 100)

The universal agent, God, instituted this measure, which is time, and He did so in accord with His will. Hence time also is to be numbered among the things produced by God. . . . Time and the things existing in time began just when God wished them to begin. (ss 103)

The continuous shining of the sun is required for the preservation of light in the air; similarly God must unceasingly confer existence on things if they are to persevere in existence. Thus all things are related to God as an object is to its maker, and this is not only so far as they begin to exist, but so far as they continue to exist. (SS 146–47)

God is one, simple, perfect, and infinite.... All these truths are assembled in a brief article of our Creed, wherein we profess to believe "in one God, almighty." (SS 33)

God will supply what is wanting. (SS 183)

God cannot render satisfaction, just as He cannot merit. Such a service pertains to one who is subject to another. Thus God was not in position to satisfy for the sin of the whole of human nature; and a mere man was unable to do so.... Hence divine Wisdom judged it fitting that God should become man, so that thus one and the same person would be able both to restore man and to offer satisfaction. (SS 229)

The reason why Christ demonstrated the truth of His resurrection and the glory of His risen body by so many proofs, was the difficulty that faith in the resurrection presents.... Further, He manifested the truth not only by visible signs, but also by proofs appealing to the intellect, such as when "He opened their understanding so that they might understand the Scriptures," and showed that according to the writings of the prophets He was to rise again. (SS 309)

There is a twofold life. One is a life of the body, imparted by the soul, and this is called the *life of nature*. The other comes from God and is called the *life of justice* or the *life of grace*. This life is given to us through faith, by which God dwells in us, according to Habakkuk 2:4: "The just shall live in his faith." (SS 310)

Faith has to do with truths that surpass the comprehension of reason. . . . One article pertains to the divine unity. For, even though we prove by reason that God is one, the fact that He governs all things directly or that He wishes to be worshiped in some particular way, is a matter relating to Faith. (SS 328–29)

Even when we have faith, there still remains in the soul an impulse toward something else, namely, the perfect vision of the truth assented to in faith, and the attainment of whatever can lead to such truth. (SS 334)

In order that a man arrive at the perfect vision of heavenly happiness, he must first of all believe God, as a disciple believes the master who is teaching him. (T 173)

The believer has sufficient motive for believing, for he is moved by the authority of Divine teaching confirmed by miracles, and, what is more, by the inward instinct of the Divine invitation. (ST 1187)

Just as man assents to first principles, by the natural light of his intellect, so does a virtuous man, by the habit of virtue, judge aright of things concerning that virtue; and in this way, by the light of faith which God bestows on him, a man assents to truths of faith and not to their contraries. (T 173)

Meditation on the divine works is indeed necessary in order to build up man's faith in God. . . . Through meditating on His works we are able somewhat to admire and consider the divine wisdom. For things made by art are illustrative of the art itself, since they bear the imprint of that art. Now God brought things into being by His wisdom. (T 174)

We must firmly maintain that the world has not always existed: catholic faith teaches it and no scientific proof can succeed in proving the opposite. (SP 265)

Everything which goes on in this world, including even what seems fortuitous and chance, must be traced back to God's providence. (SP 280)

Faith sometimes means what we believe, sometimes the act of believing, and sometimes the disposition to believe. (SP 392)

Love is born of faith and hope; for what we believe, we both hope for and love. (CA 19)

Faith is the light of the soul. (CA 63)

Even if some of the faithful lack living faith, they should endeavor to acquire it. (ST 1178)

Since the chief object of faith consists in those things which we hope to see, according to Hebrews 11:1: *Faith is the substance of things to be hoped for*, it follows that those things are in themselves of faith, which orders us directly to eternal life. (ST 1173)

Just as a man ought to perform acts of moral virtue, on account of the judgement of his reason, and not on account of a passion, so ought he to believe matters of faith, not on account of human reason, but on account of the Divine authority. (ST 1187)

Faith works through charity. Therefore the love of charity is the form of faith. . . . Faith is perfected and formed by charity. (ST 1192)

Nothing is more certain than the word of God. Therefore science is not more certain than faith; nor is anything else. (ST 1196)

Just as taking a vow is a matter of will, and keeping a vow, a matter of obligation, so acceptance of the faith is a matter of the will, whereas keeping the faith, when once one has received it, is a matter of obligation. (ST 1219)

Although God is all-powerful and supremely good, nevertheless He allows certain evils to take place in the universe, which He might prevent, lest, without them, greater goods might be forfeited, or greater evils ensue. (ST 1222)

Faith can have no mean or extremes in the point of trusting to the First Truth. . . . So too, hope has no mean or extremes, as regards its principal object, since it is impossible to trust too much in the Divine assistance. (ST 1245)

We derive from God both knowledge of truth and the attainment of perfect goodness. Accordingly faith makes us adhere to God, as the source whence we derive the knowledge of truth, since we believe that what God tells us is true. (ST 1246)

Calling Him, *Lord, Lord*, is a mark of faith. But what avails it to confess with the mouth Him whom you deny with your works? (CA 850)

Christ's Passion was sufficiently satisfactory for the sins of the whole world. (ST 2631)

To pay worship to God as Father is yet more excellent than to pay worship to God as Creator and Lord. (ST 1696)

There cannot be a greater grace than the grace of Christ. (ST 2090)

The truth of faith includes not only inward belief, but also outward profession, which is expressed not only by words, whereby one confesses the faith, but also by deeds, whereby a person shows that he has faith, according to James 2:18, *I will show thee, by works, my faith.* (ST 1719)

A Christian is one who is Christ's. Now a person is said to be Christ's, not only through having faith in Christ, but also because he is actuated to virtuous deeds by the Spirit of Christ. (ST 1719)

Just as besides the grace of faith, the grace of the word is necessary that people may be instructed in the faith, so too is the grace of miracles necessary that people may be confirmed in their faith. (ST 1925)

The measure of grace is sufficient. (ST 2074)

Christ's Passion was not only a sufficient but a super-abundant atonement for the sins of the human race. . . . The dignity of Christ's flesh is not to be estimated solely from the nature of flesh, but also from the Person assuming it—namely, inasmuch as it was God's flesh, the result of which was that it was of infinite worth. (ST 2284)

Christ made satisfaction, not by giving money or anything of the sort, but by bestowing what was of greatest price—Himself—for us. And therefore Christ's Passion is called our redemption. (ST 2286)

Christ is the fountain of life. (ST 2293)

Christ's Passion had a virtue which was neither temporal nor transitory, but everlasting, according to Hebrews 10:14, *For by one oblation He hath perfected for ever them that are sanctified.* And so it is evident that Christ's Passion had no greater efficacy then than it has now. (ST 2308)

The power of Christ's Passion is united to us by faith and the sacraments, but in different ways; because the link that comes from faith is produced by an act of the soul: whereas the link that comes from the sacraments, is produced by making use of exterior things. (ST 2360)

The entire sanctification of the sacraments is derived from Christ. . . . Christ's blessing is enough. (ST 2426)

Faith adheres to all the articles of faith by reason of one mean, viz, on account of the First Truth proposed to us in the Scriptures, according to the teaching of the Church who has the right understanding of them. Hence whoever abandons this means is altogether lacking in faith. (ST 1199)

THE SECOND GLORIOUS MYSTERY

THE ASCENSION OF JESUS INTO HEAVEN

Hope

Ask, and it will be given you; seek, and you will find; knock, and it will be opened to you.—Luke 11:9

The day of mercy is the birthday of the Lord, in which the Sun of Righteousness arises upon us, or more truly, He Who made that day so glorious. (H 3)

It is a great token of goodness that every creature conceives itself to be good; therefore, because God is good, so are we. (H 7–8)

The Lord promises three rewards to His servants: happiness, dignity and eternity. (H 12)

He so graciously receives those seeking Him. . . . He is Life, since He gives eternal life to those who are seeking Him. (H 24)

Jesus Christ procured for us by His advent the covenant of an eternal inheritance. (H 169)

"Ask, and it shall be given you; seek, and ye shall find; knock, and it shall be opened unto you." "Ask" humbly, and ye shall receive; "seek" what is profitable, and "ye shall find"; "knock" continually, and the Kingdom of Heaven shall be opened unto you. (H 30)

We should *hope* in Him above all, as if in a liberator.
(H 48)

All things naturally desire good, and tend to good. (H 120)

As God is infinite goodness, so He desires to communicate Himself by infinite gifts to all. (H 170)

"Let us make man to our own image and likeness." He did not say this of the Heavens or of the stars, but of man—not, indeed, as regards man's body, but as regards his soul, which is endowed with a free will and is incorruptible, and in which he resembles God. (C 21)

Our hope is raised, because it is evident that God's Son took our flesh and came to us not for a trifling reason, but for our exceedingly great good. He bound Himself to us, as it were, by deigning to take a human soul and body and to be born of a Virgin, in order to bestow His Godhead on us. (C 35–36)

His Passion was so efficacious that it suffices to atone for all the sins of the whole world, even of a hundred thousand worlds. (C 42)

No matter how great a man's afflictions may be, he should always hope in God's assistance and trust in Him. (C 50)

Anyone who serves God should be full of confidence. (C 50)

The Holy Spirit strengthens our hope of eternal life, inasmuch as He is a kind of surety that we shall inherit it. . . . He is, as it were, a token of eternal life. The reason is that eternal life is due to a man inasmuch as he is made a son of God. (C 75)

We call God *Father* because He has adopted us. For He endowed other creatures with trifling gifts, but to us He granted the inheritance, because (as the Apostle says) we are His sons "and if sons, heirs also." (C 109–10)

God foresaw the fall of the angel Lucifer and that of the first man. He permitted temptation; He knew in advance all the evil that would result from it for the human race, and also all the good—that is to say, the Incarnation of the Son of God, by which man receives a glory even greater than that which he had before the Fall. (W 13)

Wisdom and goodness are said to be in God, and are God Himself, as well as the divine essence. (SS 62)

God with patience and mercy awaits the sinner until his death in order to have pity upon him, should he, even in this last moment, regret his evil ways and turn toward Him. For the Lord who is merciful does not rejoice in the loss of the living. (W 21)

In the measure that a man seeks to conserve this grace and to use it for the praise of God and the common welfare, in the same measure will he receive a more abundant infusion of grace in this world and of glory in Paradise. (W 37–38)

He is true in His promises. According to God's own testimony, it is easier for Heaven and earth to pass away than that a single one of His words should change or cease to be true. For the Lord Jesus never speaks in vain, as we do, but each one of the words He has pronounced in time was said, in His wisdom, from all eternity. (W 47)

God cannot in any way be deficient in goodness. For what is essential to a being cannot be lacking. . . . It is impossible for God not to be good. We can use a more appropriate example to illustrate this: as it is impossible for a man not to be a man, so it is impossible for God not to be perfectly good. (SS 123)

The object of hope is, in one way, eternal happiness, and, in another way, the Divine assistance. . . . The Divine assistance is ready to help us. (ST 1246)

If nature aims at perpetual existence in the generation of man, much more so does God in the restoration of man. Nature's tendency toward never-ending existence comes from an impulse implanted by God. . . . Risen men will live forever. (SS 176)

Give to me, O Lord my God, understanding of You, diligence in seeking You, wisdom in finding You, discourse ever pleasing to You, perseverance in waiting for You, and confidence in finally embracing You. (P 13)

You supply us with all temporal goods. You reserve for us an eternal good. You inspire us with the beauty of creation. You appeal to us with the mercy of redemption. You promise us blessings in reward. For all these I am incapable of sufficient praise. (P 19)

The Son of God, made man, brought salvation to the human race, not only by conferring the remedy of grace but also by giving an example that cannot be ignored. . . . In Him we ought to have an example of the glory we hope for and of the virtue whereby we may merit it. (SS 269)

Any suffering of His, however slight, was enough to redeem the human race, if the dignity of the sufferer is considered. For the more exalted the person on whom suffering is inflicted, the greater the injury judged to be. . . . Since Christ is a person of infinite dignity, any suffering of His has an infinite value and so suffices for the atonement of infinitely many sins. (SS 297)

By the Passion and death of Christ and by the glory of His resurrection and ascension, we are freed from sin and death, and have received justice and the glory of immortality—the former in actual fact, the latter in hope. (SS 315)

Although Christ will show Himself [at the Judgment] in His glorious form, the marks of the Passion will appear in Him, not with disfigurement, but with beauty and splendor, so that at the sight of them the elect, who will perceive that they have been saved through the sufferings of Christ, will be filled with joy. (SS 317)

Stirrings of hope arise in the soul of the believer that by God's help he may gain possession of the goods he naturally desires, once he learns of them through faith. . . . Next after faith, the virtue of hope is necessary for the perfection of Christian living. (SS 334)

Just as an earthen vessel, if it were endowed with sense, might hope to be put to good use by the potter, so man ought to cherish the hope of being rightly provided for by God. Thus we are told in Jeremiah 18:6: "As clay is in the hand of the potter, so are you in my hand, O house of Israel." (SS 338)

How precious is the soul of man, how pleasant to God is his salvation, and how great its reward. (CA 137)

God's mercies are always greater than our troubles. (CA 150)

Faith begets hope, in so far as it enables us to appreciate the prize which God awards to the just. (ST 1203)

Hope does not trust chiefly in grace already received, but on God's omnipotence and mercy, whereby even he that has not grace, can obtain it, so as to come to eternal life. Now whoever has faith is certain of God's omnipotence and mercy. (ST 1250)

If anyone were to judge, in universal, that God's mercy is not infinite, he would be an unbeliever. (ST 1261)

Hope withdraws us from evils and induces us to seek for good things, so that when hope is given up, men rush headlong into sin, and are drawn away from good works. (ST 1261)

To hope too little in Him ... implies a depreciation of His power. (ST 1263)

There is held out to us a harvest of eternal love to be provided by God. (CA 263)

He that has charity is moved more by hope than by fear. (ST 2592)

It is not our actions, but the grace of our Redeemer, that is the principal cause of the hope of salvation. (ST 2606)

A man is repaired in an instant by Divine grace. (ST 2689)

It is the mark of a happy disposition to see good rather than evil. (ST 1650)

Confidence denotes a certain strength of hope. (ST 1733)

By considering the Divine benefits and promises, man is led to the knowledge of God's mercy and goodness.
(ST 1934)

The sin of Adam was not so far-reaching as the gift of Christ. (ST 2409)

The power of Christ's Passion . . . is the universal remedy for all sins. (ST 2409)

In God's tribunal, those who return are always received, because God is a searcher of hearts, and knows those who return in sincerity. (ST 1227–28)

The Third Glorious Mystery

The Descent of the Holy Spirit

Love of God

[Y]ou shall love the Lord your God with all your heart, and with all your soul, and with all your mind, and with all your strength.—Mark 12:30

Charity is the bond of souls. (H 31)

The possessor of charity is most dear to God, for it is of that nature that they who possess it are called dear, whence the Lord calls those living in charity the most beloved. (H 41)

We should *love* Him above all, as our highest good. (H 48)

The Lord Jesus gave to us a threefold *water*—(1) the water of Baptism for the cleansing of sins ... (2) the water of wisdom for the extinction of spiritual thirst ... (3) the refreshing water of the Holy Spirit. (H 68)

It is joy to have so many gifts of the Holy Spirit, and those twelve fruits which the Apostle enumerated ... because they more refresh the mind than can be expressed by words. (H 99)

God the Father and God the Son are They Who send God the Holy Ghost, for these breathe forth the Holy Spirit, and so the Spirit with one motion proceeds from the Father and the Son. (H 197)

It is obvious that both the Father and the Son breathe out the Holy Spirit, and so we gain an insight into the doctrine of the whole Trinity. God the Father is He Who sends, God the Son the means through Whom the Father sends, and God the Holy Ghost is He Who is sent. (H 197–98)

The word Paraclete signifies comforter or advocate; now both these offices imply especially the exercise of goodness, and goodness is a peculiar attribute of God the Holy Ghost, so He is said to be our Comforter in trouble and our Advocate in blessings. (H 198)

All the blessings of nature flow from God the Holy Ghost. (H 198)

There is no greater proof of God's love than that God the Creator became a creature, that our Lord became our Brother, and that the Son of God became the Son of man.... The very thought of this should kindle and inflame our hearts with the love of God. (C 36)

The Holy Spirit is the author of all grace, since He is the first in Whom all gifts are given *gratis*. (SS 271)

The soul's life is union with God, inasmuch as God is the life of the soul (just as the soul is the life of the body). Now, the Holy Spirit unites us to God by love, for He is Himself God's love, which is why He gives life. (C 72)

The Holy Spirit enlightens our mind, because whatever we know, it is through the Holy Spirit that we know it: "But the Holy Spirit, the Paraclete, whom the Father will send in My name, will Himself teach you all things and will bring all things to your mind, whatsoever I shall have said to you." (C 74)

Union with God consists in knowing God perfectly. For the better one is known, the more perfectly one is loved. (C 96)

It is necessary that man develop perfect strength which is, as it were, a spiritual growth. This, indeed, comes to him in the sacrament of Confirmation. It is like the strengthening the Apostles received when the Holy Spirit came upon them and confirmed them. (C 255)

Prayers, almsgiving, fasting, and pilgrimages accomplished without charity are insufficient to efface the sins of those who practice these devotions. (W 58)

Loving corresponds to love. . . . The love whereby God is loved out of charity surpasses all love. Hence it is written: *O taste and see that the Lord is sweet.* (T 183 and 215)

God is substantially in Himself as beloved in lover. Therefore the Holy Spirit, who represents the divine love to
us, is not something accidental in God, but subsists in
the divine essence just as the Father and the Son do.
And so in the rule of the Catholic Faith He is exhibited
as no less worthy of adoration and glorification than the
Father and the Son are. (SS 43–44)

The procession of love presupposes the procession of
the Word.... The first notion of the Father is paternity
and the first notion of the Son is filiation, whereas procession alone is the notion of the Holy Spirit. Accordingly, the notions constituting persons are three in
number: paternity, filiation, and procession. (SS 57)

When we profess that the Holy Spirit is God, we imply
that all things are ordained to the end of divine goodness.... The words of the Creed which express our belief
that the Holy Spirit is "the giver of life" suggest that
God moves all things. (SS 165–66)

By willing to become man, God clearly displayed the
immensity of His love for man, so that henceforth men
might serve God, no longer out of fear of death, which
the first man had scorned, but out of the love of charity.
(SS 230)

The more clearly God, the essence of goodness, is seen,
the more He must be loved. (SS 364)

The very fact that we wish to cling to God in a spiritual
fellowship pertains to reverence for God. (ST 1556)

If the goodness, beauty, and sweetness of creatures are so alluring to the minds of men, the fountain-head of the goodness of God Himself, in comparison with the rivulets of goodness which we find in creatures, will set on fire the minds of men and draw them wholly to itself. (T 175)

We are in the image of God by the fact that we exist, that we know that we exist, and that we love both this knowledge and this existence.... Loving is the perfection of love. (T 177–78)

It is through charity that one is urged to the contemplation of God.... This is the ultimate perfection of the contemplative life, namely that the divine truth be not only seen but also loved. (T 215)

The lover is not satisfied with a superficial apprehension of the beloved, but strives to gain an intimate knowledge of everything pertaining to the beloved, so as to penetrate into his very soul. Thus it is written concerning the Holy Ghost, Who is God's love, that He *searcheth all things, yea the deep things of God*. (T 283)

Will's love moves us more ardently than mind's knowledge, since knowledge assimilates but love transforms.

(SP 173)

Charity is said to be a higher virtue than any other in this life precisely because it directs everyone to God, and in heaven it will enjoy ultimate rest in God. (SP 322)

Love of supreme good as source of our natural existence exists in us by nature, but, as object of a bliss which exceeds the whole capacity of created nature, it exists in us not by nature but above nature. (SP 425)

Even obedience, and hope likewise, and whatever other virtue might precede the act of faith, is quickened by charity. . . . And consequently charity is spoken of as the form of faith. (ST 1192)

To be a foundation a thing requires not only to come first, but also to be connected with the other parts of the building: since the building would not be founded on it unless the other parts adhered to it. Now the connecting bond of the spiritual edifice is charity. . . . Consequently faith without charity cannot be the foundation. (ST 1196)

Just as the Holy Ghost directs man's will by the gift of charity, so as to move it directly to some supernatural good; so also, by the gift of understanding, He enlightens the human mind, so that it knows some supernatural truth, to which the right will needs to tend. (ST 1206)

Faith in God is perfected by love of Him. (ST 1230)

Charity, properly speaking, makes us tend to God, by uniting our affections to Him, so that we live, not for ourselves, but for God. (ST 1246)

It is evident that charity cannot remain lifeless, since it is itself the ultimate form of the virtues. (ST 1286)

The more one loves a man, the more one fears to offend him and to be separated from him. . . . This fear decreases as charity increases, chiefly as regards its act, since the more a man loves God, the less he fears punishment.

(ST 1257)

God is faithful: by Whom you are called unto the fellowship of His Son. The love which is based on this communication, is charity: wherefore it is evident that Charity is the friendship of man for God. (ST 1269)

Charity is not something created in the soul, but is the Holy Ghost Himself dwelling in the mind. . . . This movement is from the Holy Ghost. (ST 1270)

Charity attains God, it unites us to God. . . . There is no comparison with charity since it is not founded principally on the virtue of man, but on the goodness of God. (ST 1271)

Since a mother is one who conceives within herself and by another, charity is called the mother of the other virtues, because, by commanding them, it conceives the acts of the other virtues, by the desire of the last end. (ST 1275)

Charity is regulated, not by the reason, as human virtues are, but by God's wisdom, and transcends the rule of human reason, according to Ephesians 3:19: *The charity of Christ, which surpasseth all knowledge.* (ST 1276)

Since to love God is something greater than to know Him, especially in this state of life, it follows that love of God presupposes knowledge of God. (ST 1308)

The more we love God the better our love is. (ST 1309)

Man's ultimate good consists in his soul cleaving to God, according to Psalm 72:28: *It is good for me to adhere to my God.* (ST 1309)

To love God with the whole heart, is to have the heart inclined to the love of no one thing more than of God. To love God again with the whole soul is to have the mind stayed upon the truth, and to be firm in the faith. For the love of the heart and the love of the soul are different. (CA 762)

Charity is the root of all the virtues and gifts. (ST 1759)

It is charity that unites us to God, Who is the last end of the human mind, *since he that abideth in charity abideth in God, and God in him* (1 Jn. 4:16). Therefore the perfection of the Christian life consists radically in charity. (ST 1950)

Since the Holy Ghost is love drawing us up to heavenly things, therefore our Lord said to His disciples (Jn. 16:7): *It is expedient to you that I go; for if I go not, the Paraclete will not come to you; but if I go, I will send Him to you.* (ST 2328)

By Baptism man is built up into a spiritual dwelling, and is written like a spiritual letter; whereas by the sacrament of Confirmation, like a house already built, he is consecrated as a temple of the Holy Ghost, and as a letter already written, is signed with the sign of the cross. (ST 2432)

The Fourth Glorious Mystery

The Assumption of Mary into Heaven

Desire for Heaven

Come, O blessed of my Father, inherit the kingdom prepared for you from the foundation of the world.—Matthew 25:34

The day of grace is the time of grace; the day of justice is the day of judgement; the day of glory is the day of eternity. (H 3)

Eternity is a fountain of life. As St. Dionysius says, "Eternity is endless, and at the same time the whole and perfect possession of life." (H 12)

"Where I am, there also shall My servant be." Where Christ is, there is joyful exultation and eternal delightfulness, to which for His sake may the Lord God bring us. (H 12)

We ought by holiness to pass over the sea of this world to the heavenly country, to God. (H 31)

One drop [of the water of Paradise] is larger than the ocean. (H 68)

The future joys of the saints are said to consist of three things—(1) in the consolation of the Divine Presence ... (2) in the highest exultation of heart ... (3) in the attaining of eternity. (H 75)

Those who lay up treasure in heaven shall find their own delights, the granary of whom will be filled by plenty, because they shall be satiated, when His glory will be manifested. (H 86)

Our conversation is in heaven while we live on earth; because we have our hope there, and because we are like to the angels both in living and knowing. (H 146)

Love ... leads onwards to the desire of heavenly things.
(H 182)

Eternity is the possession of life, wholly and forever. (H 187)

The Godhead is an object of such delight that no one can see it without joy. (C 64)

Our natural desire for more perfect knowledge ever remains. But a natural desire cannot be in vain. (SS 116)

Since we believe that there is another, better life to which we shall come after death, it is evident that no one should fear death or do anything wrong through fear of death. (C 90)

It is fitting that the last article of Faith in the Creed should give expression to that which is the end of all our desires (namely, eternal life) in the words, *And life everlasting. Amen*. (C 95)

Since in Heaven the saints will possess God perfectly, it is evident that their desires will be satisfied and that their glory will surpass their expectations. . . . Whatever is delightful will be there superabundantly. (C 96–97)

If we desire knowledge, there will be most perfect knowledge, because we shall know all the natures of things and all truth—and whatever we wish, we shall know. We shall possess whatever we desire to possess, together with eternal life itself. (C 97–98)

Eternal life consists in perfect security. In this world there is no perfect security, since the more someone has and the higher his position, the more he has to fear and the more he wants. (C 98)

We press on toward Him as toward some distant goal. But when we see Him by direct vision we shall hold Him present within ourselves. (SS 361)

God wills that we may have eternal life, because whoever makes a certain thing for a certain purpose wills that purpose for it. God made man, but not without a purpose, for as the Psalm says, "Hast Thou made all the children of men in vain?" [v. 48]   (c 130–31)

The period of eternity exceeds the present time incomparably more than a thousand years exceeds one day.   (c 190)

The life of glory . . . is the greatest of all blessings.   (c 203)

Our desire is not satisfied until we penetrate to its essence. Therefore our natural desire for knowledge cannot come to rest within us until we know the first cause, and that not in any way, but in its very essence. This first cause is God.   (ss 117)

This ultimate end of man we call *beatitude.* For a man's happiness or beatitude consists in the vision whereby he sees God in His essence. Of course, man is far below God in the perfection of his beatitude. For God has this beatitude by His very nature, whereas man attains beatitude by being admitted to a share in the divine light.   (ss 119)

It is fitting that nature should be completely restored at the renovation of risen man, for such renovation will be accomplished directly by God, whose works are perfect.   (ss 178–79)

Man's last end consists not in spiritual acts of any sort whatever, but in the vision of God according to His essence. And God is eternal; hence the intellect must be in contact with eternity. . . . So those who enjoy the vision of God possess eternal life.   (SS 184)

There, with You, is refuge from all dangers, multitude of dwelling places, and harmony of wills. There, with You, resides the cheerfulness of spring, the brilliance of summer, the fruitfulness of autumn, and the gentle repose of winter. Give me, O Lord my God, that life without death and that joy without sorrow.   (P 55 and 57)

I also pray that You bring me, a sinner, to that ineffable banquet where You dwell with Your Son and Holy Spirit. You Who are for Your saints true light, complete fulfillment, eternal joy, consummate delight, and perfect happiness.   (P 83 and 85)

Hope presupposes desire. Before a thing can be hoped for, it must first be desired.   (SS 346)

Beatitude or happiness is nothing else than perfect good. Therefore all who share in beatitude can be happy only by participation in the divine beatitude, which is man's essential goodness. . . . We are beatified not by beholding the angels, but by seeing the Truth.   (SS 356)

The last and crowning act is the contemplation itself of the truth.   (T 199)

In the vision of the divine essence, the created spirit possesses God as present; and the vision itself sets the affections completely on fire with divine love. . . . Surely God, who is the very essence of beauty and goodness, cannot be gazed at without love. Therefore perfect vision is followed by perfect love. (SS 362–63)

In Heaven there is nothing to fear. Restlessness of craving will end, because of the full possession of all good. Every external cause of disturbance will cease, because all evil will be absent. The perfect tranquility of peace will be enjoyed there. Isaiah 32:18 alludes to this: "My people shall sit in the beauty of peace." (SS 364)

Think of whatever you can want in pleasures and delights, and the saints have all that I speak of spiritual delights, not of worldly and unclean ones. *At thy right hand are delights.* If you love riches, the saints are the most wealthy, for nothing is lacking to those who fear God; *they shall enjoy abundance.* (W 15)

What is it to eat at the table of God? It is to delight and to be refreshed with that by which God is refreshed. And what is that by which God is refreshed? It is His goodness. When you are refreshed by the goodness of God, then you are eating at the table of God, and that is the blessedness of the saints. (T 21)

We are urged to the vision of the First Principle, namely God, by the love thereof; wherefore Gregory says that the contemplative life tramples on all cares and longs to see the face of its Creator. (T 194)

God transcends the native power of all creatures and is something no creature can attain by nature. What properly measures it is eternity itself; and the seeing of God, bliss itself, is thus eternal life. (SP 332)

Desire of a goal causes desire of everything leading to the goal. So since bliss is the goal of human life, whatever it is our will's desire to do is ordered to bliss, and we see this in experience. For people desire things because they think them good; and when they possess things they think good, they reckon themselves that much closer to bliss. (SP 340)

The deep longing of the saints for the doctrine of God shall receive perfect replenishment in heaven; then *they shall be filled*. Such is the bounty of a rewarding God, that His gifts are greater than the desires of the saints. (CA 152)

Since man is ordained to supernatural happiness, . . . man needs to reach to certain higher truths, for which he requires the gift of understanding. (ST 1204)

The saints in heaven will be so full of joy, that they will have no room for sorrow; and so they will not grieve for their sins, but rather will they rejoice in the Divine mercy. (ST 2932)

All things, each in its own way, desire to attain the Divine goodness. (ST 1546)

Desire will be at rest, not only our desire for God, but all our desires: so that the joy of the blessed is full to perfection,—indeed over-full, since they will obtain more than they were capable of desiring. . . . Man enters into it, according to Matthew 25:21: *Enter into the joy of thy Lord.* (ST 1313)

The desire of the saints to know all things will be fulfilled by the mere fact of their seeing God: just as their desire to possess all good things will be fulfilled by their possessing God. . . . God suffices the affections in that He has perfect goodness, and by possessing Him we possess all goods. (ST 2968)

In order that anyone go straight along a road, he must have some knowledge of the end: thus an archer will not shoot the arrow straight unless he first see the target. (ST 2261)

The Fifth Glorious Mystery

The Crowning of Mary Queen of Heaven and Earth

Devotion to Mary

Behold, your mother!
—John 19:27

The Virgin in a wonderful way, before all the other saints, is the Temple of God. (H 169)

The Blessed Virgin had more faith, hope and charity than any other creature.... There was nothing in the Virgin which was not filled with holiness. (H 169)

She [the Blessed Virgin] instituted the life of virgins. Virginity is the sister of angels. To live in the flesh, yet not after the flesh, is to live a heavenly and not an earthly life. (H 171–72)

She was full of grace as regards her soul, in which dwelt all the plentitude of grace. For God's grace is given for two purposes: the performance of good deeds and the avoidance of evil. (C 163)

The Son of God is also the Son of a woman. (H 172)

There have been some so presumptuous as to assert that it is possible for man by his own powers to live here below without committing sin. But this has been given to none except Christ (who had the Spirit without measure) and the Blessed Virgin (who was full of grace, in whom there was no sin). (C 144)

It was not fitting that an angel should pay respect to a man until one should be found in human nature who would surpass the angels in these three ways [in dignity, close association with God, and fullness of divine grace]— and such was the Blessed Virgin. Thus, in order to show that she excelled him, the angel desired to show her reverence by saying, *Hail.* (C 163)

She surpasses the angels in her fullness of grace, which is greater in her than in any angel. To indicate this, the angel paid reverence to her by saying *full of grace*, as if to say, "I bow to thee because thou dost surpass me in fullness of grace." (C 163)

She practiced the works of *all* the virtues, while other saints were conspicuous in certain particular virtues— one for humility, another for chastity, another for mercy— for which reason each one is an example to us of some special virtue. (C 164)

The Blessed Virgin was full of grace as regards the over-flow of grace from her soul into her flesh, or body. For while it is a great thing in the saints to be so endowed with grace that their souls are holy, the soul of the Blessed Virgin was so full of grace that it overflowed into her flesh, fitting it for the conception of God's Son. (C 165)

So full of grace was the Blessed Virgin, that it over-flowed onto all mankind. It is, indeed, a great thing that any one saint has so much grace that it is conductive to the salvation of many; but it is most wondrous to have so much grace as to suffice for the salvation of all man-kind. Thus it is in Christ and in the Blessed Virgin. (C 165)

In every danger you can find a refuge in this same glo-rious Virgin. . . . Likewise, you may obtain her assis-tance in every virtuous deed. (C 165)

She is rightly called *Mary*, which signifies that in herself she is enlightened ("The Lord will fill thy soul with brightness'), and that she enlightens others throughout the world. Thus, she is compared to the sun and to the moon. (C 166)

The Blessed Virgin is more intimately associated with God than an angel is, since with her are God the Father, God the Son, and God the Holy Spirit—in a word, the whole Trinity. . . . So no greater praise could be addressed to her than that which is found in the words, *The Lord is with thee.* (C 167)

Being the Mother of our Lord she is our Lady. Consequently, she is fittingly named *Mary*, which in the Syrian tongue means "lady." (C 167)

She was immune from the curse on man and woman . . . that they would return to dust. From this also was the Blessed Virgin exempt, since she was taken up bodily into Heaven, for we believe that after her death she was raised up and carried into Heaven: *Arise, O Lord, into Thy rest: Thou and the ark which Thou didst sanctify.* (C 168)

The name *Mary* [is] proper to her, which means "star of the sea." Just as the star of the sea guides sailors to port, so Mary guides Christ's followers to heavenly glory. (C 168)

Eve in her fruit sought pleasure, since it was good to eat; yet she did not find it, for at once she perceived that she was naked, and tasted sorrow. But in the Fruit of the Blessed Virgin we find sweetness and salvation. (C 169)

Let us seek in the Virgin's Fruit that which we desire to have. This Fruit is blessed by God, because God so filled Him with all grace that it overflows upon us who bow to Him in adoration. . . . Thus is the Virgin blessed, but still more blessed is her Fruit. (C 170)

We keep the Saturdays in veneration of the Blessed Virgin, in whom remained a firm faith on that Saturday while Christ was dead. (C 189)

There would be no reason why the Son of God, bringing His body from Heaven, should have entered the Virgin's womb, if He were to receive nothing from her. . . . We must acknowledge without reservation that He came forth from the Virgin's womb in such a way that He really took His flesh from her. (SS 240)

O most blessed and sweet Virgin Mary, Mother of God, filled with all tenderness, . . . on this day and all the days of my life, I entrust to your merciful heart my body and my soul, all my acts, thoughts, choices, desires, words, deeds, my entire life and death, so that, with your assistance, all may be ordered to the good according to the will of your beloved Son, our Lord Jesus Christ. (P 21)

Since the formation of Christ's body was to be accomplished by the Holy Spirit, it behooved that woman from whom Christ took His body be filled to repletion with spiritual gifts, so that not only her soul would be endowed with virtues by the Holy Spirit, but also her womb made fruitful with divine offspring. So her soul had to be free from sin and her body far removed from every taint of carnal concupiscence. (SS 275)

She had been made more honorable and worthy than the whole world, who had carried in her womb Him whom the whole world could not contain. (CA 58)

Just as any woman is a mother from the fact that her child's body is derived from her, so the Blessed Virgin Mary ought to be called the Mother of God if the body of God is derived from her. . . . All who admit that human nature was assumed by the Son of God into the unity of His person, must admit that the Blessed Virgin Mary is the Mother of God. (SS 277)

Everything pertaining to the idea of mother is verified in the Blessed Virgin Mary. (SS 277)

The Blessed Virgin Mary became the mother of God's Son by conceiving of the Holy Spirit. Therefore it was fitting that she should be adorned with the highest degree of purity, that she might be made conformable to such a Son. And so we are to believe that she was free from every stain of actual sin—not only of mortal sin but of venial sin. (SS 278)

Freedom from sin can pertain to none of the saints after Christ, as we know from 1 John 1:8: "If we say that we have no sin we deceive ourselves, and the truth is not in us." But what is said in the Song of Solomon 4:7, "Thou art all fair, O my love, and there is not a spot in thee," can well be understood of the Blessed Virgin, Mother of God. (SS 278–79)

If Mary was thus strengthened against every movement of sin by her first sanctification, much more did grace grow in her. . . . She had been made the shrine of the Holy Spirit and the tabernacle of the Son of God. (SS 281–82)

The Child was not born for the mother, but the mother prepared for the Child. (CA 79)

She is called a *virgin* without any qualification, for she remained a virgin before the birth, at the birth, and after the birth of Christ. That there was no impairment of her virginity before and after Christ's birth is clear. . . . Christ's body, which appeared to the disciples when the doors were closed, could by the same power come forth from the closed womb of His mother. (SS 283)

It was the Blessed Virgin who said: *He hath done great things to me*, meaning the greatest of miracles that in her womb God should become man, and that she, a virgin, should bear a child. (T 6)

It pleased Him to take flesh of the womb of a woman.

(CA 35)

His mother immaculate, His mother incorrupt, His mother pure. His mother! Whose mother? The mother of God, of the Only-begotten, of the Lord, of the King, of the Maker of all things, and the Redeemer of all.

(CA 40–41)

The Blessed Virgin is said to have merited to bear the Lord of all; not that she merited His Incarnation, but because by the grace bestowed upon her she merited that grade of purity and holiness, which fitted her to be the Mother of God. (ST 2043)

She is the Mother of God. . . . The honor given to the Mother reflects on her Son, because the Mother is to be honored for her Son's sake. (ST 2157)

After Christ, who, as the universal Savior of all, needed not to be saved, the purity of the Blessed Virgin holds the highest place. (ST 2165)

We must say that the Blessed Virgin is called the Mother of God, not as though she were the Mother of the God-head, but because she is the mother, according to His human nature, of the Person who has both the divine and the human nature. (ST 2206)

It is quite enough to ascribe to the Blessed Virgin perfect virtue and abundant grace. (ST 2166)

The Son of God, who is the *Divine Wisdom* (1 Cor. 1:24) dwelt in her, not only in her soul but in her womb. And it is written (Wis. 1:4): *Wisdom will not enter into a malicious soul, nor dwell in a body subject to sins*. We must therefore confess simply that the Blessed Virgin committed no actual sin. (ST 2167)

Full indeed of grace: for to others it is given in portions; whereas on Mary the fulness of grace was showered all at once. (ST 2168)

In order to show that there is a certain spiritual wedlock between the Son of God and human nature ... in the Annunciation the Virgin's consent was besought in lieu of that of the entire human nature. (ST 2179)

Although the Blessed Virgin had no uncleanness, yet she wished to fulfil observance of purification, not because she needed it, but on account of the precept of the Law. Thus the Evangelist says pointedly that the days of her purification *according to the Law* were accomplished; for she needed no purification in herself. (ST 2222)

Through eating the fruit, Eve did not become like God, but unlike Him, since by sinning she turned away from God, her salvation, and was expelled from Paradise. On the other hand, the Blessed Virgin found likeness to God in the Fruit of her womb—and so do all the followers of Christ. (C 169)

THE
LUMINOUS
MYSTERIES

The First Luminous Mystery

The Baptism of Jesus in the Jordan

Baptism

Anyone who drinks the water that I shall give will never be thirsty again; the water that I shall give will turn into a spring inside him, welling up to eternal life.
—John 4:14

When we are baptized, we begin by confessing our Faith when we are asked, "Do you believe in God?" For Baptism is the first of the sacraments of faith. Hence our Lord said, "He that believeth and is baptized, shall be saved" since without faith, Baptism is of no avail. (C 5)

Baptism is . . . a spiritual regeneration. Just as a man cannot live in the flesh unless he is born in the flesh, so he cannot have the spiritual life of grace unless he is born again spiritually. This regeneration is effected by Baptism. (C 84)

This sacrament derives its efficacy from Christ's Passion: "All we who are baptized in Christ Jesus, are baptized in His death." For this reason, just as Christ was three days in the tomb, so Baptism is conferred by a triple immersion. (C 84)

The sacraments of the New Law . . . both contain grace and confer it. A sacrament of the New Law is a visible form of invisible grace. Thus, the exterior washing which takes place when water is poured in Baptism represents that interior cleansing which takes away sin by virtue of the sacrament of Baptism. (C 254)

The minister of Baptism ordinarily is the priest, whose office it is to baptize. In case of necessity, however, not only a deacon but also a layperson (even a pagan or a heretic) can baptize as long as he observes the form specified by the Church and intends to act according to the intention of the Church. (C 259)

The effect of Baptism is to remit both actual sin and Original Sin as well as all guilt and punishment which they incur. . . . Those who die immediately after Baptism are admitted to the glory of God without delay. Therefore the effect of Baptism is the opening of the gates of Paradise. (C 260)

Let us keep faithfully the baptismal promises that our godparents made in our name, and which oblige us to persevere in the Catholic Faith, to renounce the Devil and all his works, and to keep the Ten Commandments.

(W 49)

Whoever receives the benefit of being born again in Christ takes no small step upwards. It is not a little thing to be clothed upon with Christ and to be conformed to Him: *As many of you as have been baptized in Christ have put on Christ.* (T 7)

Who doubts that the baptism of Christ has a benefit for infants? He who at His birth had Angels to proclaim Him, the heavens to testify, and Magi to worship Him, could surely have prevented that these [holy innocents] should not have died for Him, had He not known that they died not in that death, but rather lived in higher bliss. (CA 82)

The Savior willed to be baptized not that He might Himself be cleansed, but to cleanse the water for us. From the time that [Christ] was dipped in the water, from that time has He washed away all our sins in water. (CA 108–9)

All who are worthily baptized in Christ, straightaway ascend from the water; that is, make progress in virtues, and are carried on towards a heavenly dignity. (CA 111)

As to all those who by baptism are born again, the door of the kingdom of heaven is opened, so all in baptism receive the gifts of the Holy Spirit. (CA 112)

Morally, a vineyard has been let out to each of us to dress, when the mystery of baptism was given to us, to be cultivated by action. (CA 734)

Christ after He has been once born among men, is born a second time in the sacraments, that as we adore Him then born of a pure mother, so we may now receive Him immersed in pure water. . . . That Holy Spirit which was present to Him in the womb, now shone round Him in the water, He who then made Mary pure, now sanctifies the waters. (CA 112–13)

After the washing of water the Holy Spirit descends on us from the heavenly gates, on us also is shed an unction of heavenly glory, and an adoption to be the sons of God, pronounced by the Father's voice. (CA 114–15)

Faith, which is born of the water of baptism, is tossed in the midst of the waves of this life and yet lives. (CA 275)

In the baptism of Christ is shown the working of the whole Trinity; there was the Son incarnate, the Holy Ghost appearing in the figure of a dove, and the Father made known by the voice. (CA 605)

Baptism imprints a character on the soul. . . . Baptism confers justification in virtue of the deed which is not man's deed but God's. (ST 2619)

When a man enters the Church by Baptism, he is admitted to two things, viz. the body of the faithful and the participation of the sacraments; and this latter presupposes the former, since the faithful are united together in the participation of the sacraments. (ST 2641)

Baptism does not require a movement of the free-will, because it is given chiefly as a remedy for original sin, which, in us, is not taken away by a movement of the free-will. (ST 2676)

Although in Baptism there is conferred a spiritual power to receive the other sacraments, for which reason it imprints a character, nevertheless this is not its principal effect, but the inward cleansing. (ST 2680)

In a case of necessity anyone may baptize. . . . The Baptism of desire would supply the lack of the sacrament.
(ST 1625)

As the sin of Adam reaches others only by carnal generation, so, too, the merit of Christ reaches others only by spiritual regeneration, which takes place in Baptism; wherein we are incorporated with Christ, . . . it is by grace that it is granted to man to be incorporated with Christ. And thus man's salvation is from grace. (ST 2135)

As is related in Genesis 17, Abraham received from God and at the same time both his name and the commandment of circumcision. For this reason it was customary among the Jews to name children on the very day of circumcision, as though before being circumcised they had not as yet perfect existence: just as now also children receive their names in Baptism. (ST 2220–21)

Christ was baptized, not that He might be cleansed, but that He might cleanse. (ST 2228)

The rite of Baptism was not from men, but from God, who by an interior revelation of the Holy Ghost sent John to baptize.... By the Baptism of the New Law men are baptized inwardly by the Holy Ghost, and this is accomplished by God alone. (ST 2224)

It belongs of necessity to Christ's Baptism that it be given not only in water, but also in the Holy Ghost, according to John 3:5, *Unless a man be born of water and the Holy Ghost, he cannot enter the kingdom of God.* (ST 2227)

Christ did not need spiritual Baptism, since He was filled with the grace of the Holy Ghost from the beginning of His conception.... *By going to John to be baptized by him, He sanctified baptism.* (ST 2229)

By Christ's being baptized at the perfect age, we are given to understand that Baptism brings forth perfect men. (ST 2230)

When Christ was baptized, heaven was opened, to show that in [the] future the heavenly power would sanctify Baptism. (ST 2231)

The entrance to the heavenly kingdom was opened to us by the Baptism of Christ in a special manner, which entrance had been closed to the first man through sin. Hence, when Christ was baptized, the heavens were opened, to show that the way to heaven is open to the baptized. (ST 2231)

The Holy Ghost descended visibly, under a bodily shape, on Christ at His Baptism, in order that we may believe Him to descend invisibly on all those who are baptized.

(ST 2233)

The Holy Ghost appeared under the form of a dove on account of the proper effect of Baptism, which is the remission of sins and reconciliation with God: for the dove is a gentle creature. (ST 2233)

After His Passion and resurrection He made Baptism obligatory, not only on the Jews, but also on the Gentiles, when He gave the commandment: *Going, teach ye all nations.* (ST 2381)

Water flowed from Christ's side to wash us; blood, to redeem us. Wherefore blood belongs to the sacrament of the Eucharist, while water belongs to the sacrament of Baptism. Yet this latter sacrament derives its cleansing virtue from the power of Christ's blood. (ST 2382)

This white garment is given, ... as a sign of the glorious resurrection, unto which men are born again by Baptism; and in order to designate the purity of life, to which he will be bound after being baptized, according to Romans 6:4, *That we may walk in newness of life.* (ST 2390)

The perfect conversion to God is of those who are regenerated in Christ by Baptism. Therefore Baptism should not be deferred from day to day. (ST 2400)

Baptism, by the grace which it bestows, removes not only past sins, but hinders the commission of future sins. (ST 2401)

The teacher enlightens outwardly and ministerially by catechizing: but God enlightens the baptized inwardly, by preparing their hearts for the reception of the doctrines of truth. (ST 2412)

As the child while in the mother's womb receives nourishment not independently, but through the nourishment of its mother, so also children before the use of reason, being as it were in the womb of their mother the Church, receive salvation not by their own act, but by the act of the Church. (ST 2405)

Bodily health is not the essential effect of Baptism, but a miraculous work of Divine providence. (ST 2414)

The sacrament of Baptism is the work of God, not of man. (ST 2416)

The protecting pillar of cloud and the crossing of the Red Sea were indeed figures of our Baptism, whereby we are born again of water, signified by the Red Sea; and of the Holy Ghost, signified by the pillar of cloud. (ST 2416)

THE SECOND LUMINOUS MYSTERY

THE WEDDING AT CANA

Marriage and Family Life

Every sound tree bears good fruit, but the bad tree bears evil fruit.—Matthew 7:17

In literal marriages there should be present three good qualities: (1) faith, that the marriage bed not be violated ... (2) offspring, that children may be generated for the Lord ... (3) an oath, that neither can be separated the one from the other. (H 26)

Power is conferred in the sacrament of Confirmation. Therefore, those who have charge of children ought to be most careful to see that they are confirmed, because great grace is bestowed in Confirmation. (C 85)

Among those to whom we are bound to do good are those in some way united to us. Thus, "If any man have not care of his own and especially of those of his house, he hath denied the Faith." Now, among all our relatives, there are none closer than our father and mother.... Hence, God has given us the commandment: "*Honor thy father and thy mother.*" (C 199–200)

Parents, therefore, should give instruction without delay to their children because "a young man according to his way, even when he is old, will not depart from it." (C 200–1)

Since we owe our birth to our parents, we ought to honor them more than any other superiors, because from those others we receive only temporal things. . . . In doing this, you shall also honor yourself. (C 201)

Since we receive nourishment from our parents in our childhood, we must support them in their old age. (C 201)

We must obey our parents, for they have instructed us. "Children, obey your parents in all things." This excepts, of course, those things which are contrary to God. (C 202)

Honor thy father and thy mother. Among all the Commandments, this one only has the additional words: *that thou mayest be long-lived upon the land.* The reason for this is lest it be thought that there is no reward for those who honor their parents, seeing that it is a natural obligation. Hence it must be known that the five most desirable rewards are promised to those who honor their parents. (C 202–3)

A father naturally treasures his children, but the contrary is not always the case: "He that honoreth his father shall have joy in his own children." (C 204)

Adultery is forbidden. This is fitting, since husband and wife are as one body: "They shall be," says the Lord, "two in one flesh." (C 221)

Marriage is contracted before the eyes of the Church and thereupon God is called, as it were, to witness a bond of fidelity which must be kept: "The Lord hath been witness between thee and the wife of thy youth." (C 222)

If you ask from your wife what you do not keep yourself, then you are unfaithful. (C 223)

It must be known that this Commandment [Thou shalt not commit adultery] does not merely forbid adultery, but also every form of immodesty and impurity. (C 225)

When it is had with the intention of bringing forth offspring, married intercourse is an act of virtue. (C 225)

The threefold good of Matrimony includes: a. The birth of children and their education to the worship of God; b. Fidelity, which one spouse must render to the other; and c. Its sacramental character. The indivisibility of Matrimony shows forth the indivisible union of Christ and His Church. (C 268)

The husband ought to go before the wife in virtue. It is a shame for the husband to say that this is impossible. Why not the husband as well as the wife? (CA 184)

The Lord who brought peace and goodwill on earth, would have it reign especially in the matrimonial bond. (CA 189)

A child is by nature part of its father: thus, at first, it is not distinct from its parents as to its body, so long as it is enfolded within its mother's womb; and later on after birth, and before it has the use of its free-will, it is enfolded in the care of its parents, which is like a spiritual womb. (ST 1223)

It is the parents' duty to look after the salvation of their children, especially before they come to the use of reason. (ST 1223)

A mother, whose love is the greatest, seeks rather to love than to be loved. (ST 1305)

No benefactor confers a benefit equal to that which a man receives from his parents: wherefore in paying back benefits received, we should give the first place to our parents before all others. (ST 1323)

The Lord Himself, who has filled the souls of mothers with affection for their offspring, will more readily listen to their desires. (CA 691)

Just as a man ought to bestow temporal favors on those especially of whom he has temporal care, so too ought he to confer spiritual favors, such as correction, teaching and the like, on those who are entrusted to his spiritual care. (ST 1335)

They ought to be joined one and one, and never put asunder; And he said, *For this cause shall a man leave his father and his mother, and shall cleave to his wife*. In like manner He says *his wife*, and not *wives*. (CA 652)

He is cruel and unjust who puts away a chaste wife.

(CA 656)

If he that offers his food in prayer to God eats it sanctified, for it is sanctified by the word of God, and by prayer, as the Apostle speaks, how much rather ought children to be offered to God, and sanctified? (CA 661)

The character of parents is a witness to the sons; if the father be good and the mother bad, or the reverse, the children may follow sometimes one, sometimes the other. But when both are the same, it very rarely happens that bad sons spring of good parents, or the reverse, though it be so sometimes. (CA 790)

In regard to a *good life in general* as regards the conduct of the household, ... above all a virtuous life is required.

(ST 1408)

When it is impossible to repay the equivalent, it suffices to repay what one can, as in the case of honor due to God and our parents. (ST 1456)

Man's nature inclines to matrimony. . . . Holy Writ states that there has been matrimony from the beginning of the human race. (ST 2711–12)

Before sin matrimony was instituted by God, when He fashioned a helpmate for man out of his rib, and said to them: *Increase and multiply. . . .* The institution of marriage was from God. (ST 2716)

The joining of husband and wife by matrimony is the greatest of all joinings, since it is a joining of soul and body, wherefore it is called a *conjugal* union. (ST 2724)

Faith and offspring may be considered as in their principles, so that *offspring* denote the intention of having children, and *faith* the duty of remaining faithful, and there can be no matrimony without these also, since they are caused in matrimony by the marriage compact itself. (ST 2739)

The indissolubility of marriage belongs to the truth of life. (ST 2753)

According to the natural law whatever is an obstacle to the good of the offspring is an impediment to marriage. (ST 2759)

The accidental end of marriage is the binding together of mankind and the extension of friendship: for a husband regards his wife's kindred as his own. (ST 2759)

Disparity of worship is contrary to marriage in respect of its chief good, which is the good of the offspring . . . since the parents endeavor to draw their children in different directions. (ST 2783–84)

Unbelief and adultery are on a par. (ST 2785)

Fornication is directly opposed to the good of marriage, since by it the certainty of offspring is destroyed, faith is broken, and marriage ceases to have its signification when the body of one spouse is given to several others. (ST 2793)

Although the husband is the head of the wife, he is her pilot as it were, and is no more her judge than she is his. (ST 2796)

Since marriage is chiefly directed to the good of the offspring, all use of marriage which is intended for the good of the offspring is in order. (ST 2802)

To make use of sexual intercourse on account of its inherent pleasure, without reference to the end for which nature intended it, is to act against nature, as also is it if the intercourse be not such as may fittingly be directed to that end. (ST 2811)

One ought to show kindness to those especially who are by any tie whatever united to us. (ST 1497)

Since the offspring is the common good of husband and wife, the dictate of the natural law requires the latter to live together for ever inseparably: and so the indissolubility of marriage is of natural law. . . . The indissolubility of marriage is contained among the first precepts of the natural law. (ST 2818–19)

Parents and masters should be honored, on account of their having a share of the dignity of God Who is the Father and Lord of all. The aged should be honored, because old age is a sign of virtue, though this sign fail at times. (ST 1465)

The principles of our being and government are our parents and our country, that have given us birth and nourishment. Consequently man is debtor chiefly to his parents and his country, after God. (ST 1632)

A long life is promised to those who honor their parents not only as to the life to come, but also as to the present life. (ST 1703)

That which regards nature should be nourished and fostered in children, but that which pertains to the lack of reason in them should not be fostered, but corrected. (ST 1773)

It is evident that the upbringing of a human child requires not only the mother's care for his nourishment, but much more the care of his father as guide and guardian, and under whom he progresses in goods both internal and external. (ST 1816)

Just as it belongs to the woman to be subject to her husband in matters relating to the family life, so it belongs to the husband to provide the necessaries of that life. (ST 1868)

Nothing hinders a creature from receiving from God a gift of grace at the very beginning of its creation. In this way did Christ's soul in the first instant of its creation receive grace ... He was in the state of beatitude from the very beginning. (ST 2202–3)

Little children and novices need more than ordinary care. Consequently someone is needed to receive the baptized from the sacred font as though for the purpose of instructing and guiding them. (ST 2397)

Children while in the mother's womb have not yet come forth into the world to live among other men. . . . They can, however, be subject to the action of God, in Whose sight they live, so as, by a kind of privilege, to receive the grace of sanctification; as was the case with those who were sanctified in the womb. (ST 2407)

THE THIRD LUMINOUS MYSTERY

THE PROCLAMATION OF THE KINGDOM OF GOD

The Kingdom of God

Yes, I am a king. I was born for this, I came into the world for this: to bear witness to the truth; and all who are on the side of truth listen to my voice.—John 18:37

We rise to a new and glorious life by avoiding whatever was an occasion or a cause of death and sin.... This new life is the life of righteousness which renews the soul and brings us to the life of glory. (C 57)

Now is the time for mercy, whereas the time to come will be the time for justice only. Thus the present time is ours, but the future will be God's alone. (C 68)

We need to bear in mind that He is near to us, nay, within us, since He is said to be in the heavens, i.e., in the saints who are called *the heavens*. (C 117)

God's name is lovable: "There is no other name under Heaven given among men whereby we must be saved", and we should all desire to be saved. (C 119)

The result (of the coming of the kingdom) will be the destruction of death. Since Christ is life, in His kingdom there can be no death since it is contrary to life. Thus it is said: "Last of all, the enemy, death, shall be destroyed." This will be fulfilled at the resurrection. (C 125)

In this world, however, there are many things contrary to the salvation of mankind. When, therefore, we pray *Thy kingdom come*, we ask to be made partakers of the heavenly kingdom and of the glory of Paradise. (C 125)

This kingdom is desirable because of its perfect liberty. Although all men desire liberty naturally, here there is none; but in Heaven there is perfect liberty without any trace of bondage. . . . In fact, not only will all be free, but all will be kings. (C 126)

All shall be of one will with God: whatever the saints will, God shall will; and whatever God wills, the saints shall will. . . . In this way, all will reign, since the will of all will be done, and God shall be the crown of all: "In that day shall the Lord of hosts be for a crown of glory and for a diadem of beauty unto the residue of His people." (C 126)

Let God reign in your heart. . . . This is when you are ready to obey God and keep all His commandments. Thus, when we ask that His kingdom may come, we pray that God (and not sin) may reign in us. (C 127)

If you await the coming of His kingdom, i.e., the glory of Paradise, you have no need to regret the loss of earthly goods. (C 128)

When a thing attains the end for which it was made, it is said to be saved, whereas when it fails to reach that end it is said to be lost. Now, God made man for eternal life; and consequently, when man obtains eternal life, he is saved, which is God's will. . . . This will is already fulfilled in the angels and saints, who are in Heaven, who see, know, and enjoy God. (C 131)

Of all desirable things the first place belongs to that which is most lovable. This is God, and therefore you seek first the glory of God by saying, *Hallowed be Thy name.* (C 159)

It was because the holy Fathers saw the good things which were about to happen at His Advent that they were calling with so great desire, "O that thou wouldst rend the heavens and come down." . . . Let us, therefore, ask that this Lord and King may come to us. (H 6–7)

For a very small servitude He gives eternal life and the heavenly kingdom, and such a Lord is without doubt to be rejoiced in. Who saves His servants by redeeming them; Who dismisses all their debts by justifying them; and Who will crown them with an eternal kingdom by preserving them. (H 15)

It is the time for seeking the Lord (Hos. 10:12), "It is time to seek the Lord, till he come and rain righteousness upon you." (H 45)

They who are so the sheep shall doubtless come to the fold of Christ, which is the Kingdom of Heaven. (H 73)

Christ came forth from the Father for three reasons—(1) that He might manifest the Father in the world ... (2) to declare His Father's will to us ... (3) that He might show the Father's love towards us. (H 80)

[The just] ought to produce much fruit—charity, joy, peace, patience, long suffering, goodness, gentleness, mildness, faith, modesty, continency and chastity.... The goodness of these fruits is manifest, because by such fruits the kingdom of God is gained. (H 101)

Every other kingdom shall cease; the kingdom of Christ will remain for ever. (H 154)

The Lord promises four rewards for those who follow Him. The *first* is brightness of life.... The *second* is the power of judgment.... The *third* is a heavenly treasure.... The *fourth* is a delightful dwelling place. (H 192)

I seek out what the Good Thief sought. (P 69)

He that gave Himself to man, how shall He not give them the fellowship of His kingdom? (CA 691)

Since the one whom the king places at His right hand is judged to be the most powerful man in the kingdom, the Son of God is rightly said to sit at the Father's right hand even according to His human nature, as being exalted in rank above every creature of the heavenly kingdom. (SS 313)

Christ sits at the right hand of God according to His human nature, inasmuch as He receives judicial power from the Father. And this power He exercises even now before all His enemies are clearly seen to lie prostrate at His feet. He Himself bore witness to this fact shortly after His resurrection, in Matthew 28:18: "All power is given to me in Heaven and on Earth." (SS 317)

Christ merited the power to judge and men who have been conformed to His Passion are admitted into the company of His glory, as we are told by the Apostle in 2 Timothy 2:12: "If we suffer, we shall also reign with Him." (SS 326)

Since the notion of perfect beatitude requires that God be known and loved in Himself so that the soul embraces other objects only through Him, God reigns truly and perfectly in the good. (SS 358)

The kingdom we have been discussing is perfect happiness, for it contains all good in changeless abundance. And, since happiness is naturally desired by men, the kingdom of God, too, is desired by all. (SS 365)

He says, *the kingdom of heaven is at hand*; that is, the blessings of the heavenly kingdom. As if He had said, Prepare yourselves by repentance, for the time of eternal reward is at hand. (CA 135)

The kingdom of God will come whether we desire it or not. But herein we kindle our desires towards the kingdom, that it may come to us, and that we may reign in it. (CA 226)

The kingdom of God may stand for Christ Himself, whom we day by day wish to come, and for whose advent we pray that it may be quickly manifested to us. As He is our resurrection, because in Him we rise again, so may He be called the kingdom of God, because we are to reign in Him. (CA 226)

He who has renounced the world, is superior to its honors and to its kingdom; and hence he who dedicates himself to God and to Christ, longs not for the kingdom of earth, but for the kingdom of Heaven. (CA 226)

The weakening of the kingdom of the Devil is the increase of the kingdom of God.... He seeks to hold men's souls in captivity, the Lord to set them free; he preaches idols, the Lord the knowledge of the true God; he draws men to sin, the Lord calls them back to virtues. (CA 451 and 453)

God's majesty is infinite. (ST 3008)

Nothing save mortal sin excludes one from the kingdom of God. (ST 1512)

The will of God tends chiefly to this—that we come to the knowledge of His holiness and to reign together with Him. (ST 1545)

To be a *glorious Church not having spot or wrinkle* is the ultimate end to which we are brought by the Passion of Christ. Hence this will be in heaven, and not on earth. (ST 2077)

Because by nature Christ is God and the Son of God, the Divine glory and lordship of all things are due to Him, as to the first and supreme Lord. (ST 2135)

[God is] a merciful King; a just King; a wise King; a terrible King; an omnipotent King; an eternal King ... wisdom in the Creator, mercy in the pitiful, goodness in the good, justice in the just, severity in the terrible, power in the powerful, eternity in the eternal. This is the King. (H 5)

He is our leader, inasmuch as He ascended in order to lead us there. . . . And He ascended in order to assure us of possession of the heavenly kingdom: "I go to prepare a place for you." (C 62)

Christ will appear at the Judgment, not in humility—which belonged to the time of merit—but in the glorious form that is indicative of His reward.... The sight of His glory will be a joy to the elect who have loved Him; to these is made the promise in Isaiah 33:17, that they "shall see the King in His beauty." (SS 316)

Man can reach that [heavenly] kingdom. Otherwise it would be hoped for and prayed for in vain. In the first place, the divine promise makes this possibility clear. Our Lord says, in Luke 12:32: "Fear not, little flock, for it hath pleased your Father to give you a kingdom." (SS 366)

The perfect enlightenment will come about at Christ's second coming, ... then also shall be Christ's greatest exaltation. (ST 2275)

A man whose brother is king in a far distant country will have a great longing to go to him, to be with and stay with him. Thus, seeing that Christ is our brother, we should long to be with Him and to be united to Him. (C 36–37)

Those who have been redeemed will exult in the glory of their Redeemer. And as Christ is said to sit at God's right hand ... so at the Judgment the just are said to stand at Christ's right, as being entitled to the most honorable place near Him. (SS 326)

What ravishment will it not be to behold the King in His proper beauty, and to mingle in the choir of the Angels, and of all the saints? (CA 603)

The kingdom of heaven is the preaching of the Gospel; and the knowledge of the Scriptures which leads to life. (CA 502)

The crossing of the Red Sea foreshadowed Baptism in this—that Baptism washes away sin: whereas the crossing of the Jordan foreshadows it in this—that it opens the gate to the heavenly kingdom: and this is the principal effect of Baptism, and accomplished through Christ alone. And therefore it was fitting that Christ should be baptized in the Jordan rather than in the sea. (ST 2231)

Baptism is spiritual regeneration; inasmuch as a man dies to the old life, and begins to lead the new life. Whence it is written (Jn. 3:5): *Unless a man be born again of water and the Holy Ghost, He cannot enter into the kingdom of God.* (ST 2388)

The Holy Church is likened to a net, because it is given into the hands of fishers, and by it each man is drawn into the heavenly kingdom out of the waves of this present world, that he should not be drowned in the depth of eternal death. (CA 515)

It is like a furnace, this love of God, Who, in the banquet of regenerating grace gives unceasingly, through the ministry of His priests, His own flesh to be eaten and His own precious blood to be drunk by them who are His own sons and the heirs of the kingdom He has promised to those that love Him. (T 24)

The priest's act does not bear immediately on the kingdom, but on the sacraments, by means of which man
wins to the kingdom. (ST 2604)

The saints in their home in heaven have glory and honor.
They are all kings: in the words of the Apocalypse: Thou
hast made us kings; we are to our God a kingdom. That
glory is promised to the humble. (T 20–21)

The Fourth Luminous Mystery

The Transfiguration of Christ

The Light of Christ

I am the light of the world; anyone who follows me will not be walking in the dark; he will have the light of life.
—John 8:12

Heaven was due to Christ according to His nature, for it is natural for a thing to return to the place where it originated. Now, Christ drew His origin from God who is above all. (C 60–61)

Contemplat[e] heavenly things, for a man is wont to turn his thoughts more often toward where his father is and where the things he loves are: "Wheresoever thy treasure is, there also is thy heart." "Our conversation is in Heaven." (C 114)

In no law are such rewards promised as in the law of Christ. To the Mohammedans are promised rivers flowing with milk and honey; to the Jews, the Promised Land; but to Christians, the glory of the angels. . . . It was with this in mind that St. Peter asked: "Lord, to whom shall we go? Thou hast the words of eternal life." (C 178)

By our works we confess God's name when our actions show forth His glory: "That they may see your good works and may glorify your Father who is in Heaven." (C 184)

O how great will be that happiness where there will be no evil; where no good will be hidden; it will be intent upon eternal praises, and God will be all in all. (H 87)

This is our reward, that we may have the likeness of the resurrection of Christ. (H 95)

There will be then all beauty in our bodies, . . . when it is conformed to the body of the glory of Christ. (H 95)

A miracle is a manifest act of the power of God directed to the highest aim . . . a sign of infinite power: "And many other signs truly did Jesus in the presence of His disciples, which are not written in this book: but these are written, that ye might believe that Jesus is the Christ, the Son of God; and that believing, ye might have life through His Name" (Jn. 20:30–31). (H 153)

The sharp-sightedness of an eagle is proverbial, because it can look on the brightest light, such as the disk of the sun, and see also when it is flying aloft very remote objects, as a hare on the ground. So St. John saw the entire disk of the sun, *i.e.*, Jesus Christ in the Father, "In the beginning was the Word" (Jn. 1:1). (H 159–60)

"He that followeth Me shall not walk in darkness, but shall have the light of life"; to which may Christ Himself, the Light and the Life, bring us. (H 71)

So great is the joyousness of the Divine countenance that no one can ever look upon it without love. (H 186)

The Sun is Christ Who illumines this day with the light of glory. . . . As the true sun returning to the earth, He illumined it with His glory. (H 194)

God united human nature and the divine nature in the person of the Word, the greatest work of all. (W 23)

In God, there is a primary perfection, which is that He never changes in His nature. God Himself declares this by the prophet, "I am God and I do not change," and by Saint James: "Every best gift, and every perfect gift, is from above, coming down from the Father of lights, with whom there is no change, nor shadow of alteration." (W 5)

He carried wisdom to its summit when He conquered the devil through that wood by means of which the devil had triumphed—that is, when He hid until the end the divine power under the fragility of humanity. (W 69)

The faithful soul should try with all its effort to model itself as much as is possible on the divine ways of which we have been speaking.... From this moment on, it behooves the faithful soul to exult in joy, for it will possess these ways of God in life eternal, "when we shall be like unto Him and we shall see Him as He is." (w 77)

The Divine Word that is in God, ... has the same existence as God, whose Word He is. Consequently the Word must be of the same essence and nature as God Himself, and all attributes whatsoever that are predicated of God, must pertain also to the Word of God. (ss 38)

This we call the light of glory, whereby our intellect is perfected by God, who alone by His very nature has this form properly as His own. In somewhat the same way the disposition which heat has for the form of fire can come from the fire alone. This is the light that is spoken of in Psalm 35:10: "In Thy light we shall see light." (ss 118)

God is a cause that is completely hidden from us. Therefore, when some effect is wrought by Him outside the order of secondary causes known to us, it is called simply a miracle.... To act in this way, outside the order of secondary causes, is possible for God alone, who is the founder of this order and is not confined to it. (ss 153)

There is no other person in Christ but the eternal person, who is the person of the Son of God.... The Son of God is eternal. (ss 248)

In supernatural acts, possible and impossible are regarded from the standpoint of divine power, not from the standpoint of natural power. The fact that a blind man can be made to see or that a dead man can rise, is owing not to natural power but to divine power. But the gifts of grace are supernatural. (SS 163–64)

God, by the fact that He exists, is truth. So the intellect that sees God must rejoice in the vision of Him. Besides, God is goodness itself, which is the cause of love. So God's goodness must be loved by all who apprehend it. (SS 186)

In the final state that comes after the resurrection, all such defects will be eliminated from man. Men will no longer need food to eat, since they will be incorruptible.... Nor will men need garments to cover their nakedness, because they will be clothed with the radiance of glory. (SS 190)

The divine power, because of its infinity, is infinite and incomprehensible, the way Christ united human nature to Himself, as a sort of organ to effect man's salvation, is beyond human expression and surpasses every other union of God with creatures. (SS 246–47)

As there are two natures in Christ, there must also be two generations or births: one that is eternal, whereby He received divine nature from His Father, and the one that occurred in time, whereby He received human nature from His mother. (SS 249)

When Christ touched a leper, the action belonged to His human nature; but the fact that the touch cured the man of his leprosy is owing to the power of the divine nature. In this way all the human actions and sufferings of Christ were efficacious for our salvation in virtue of His divinity. (SS 251)

Perfect knowledge of God is effected by the light of wisdom, which is the knowledge of divine truth. Therefore the incarnate Word of God had to be perfect in grace and in the wisdom of truth. Hence we read in John 1:14: "The Word was made flesh, and dwelt among us; and we saw His glory, the glory as it were of the only begotten of the Father, full of grace and truth." (SS 254)

Christ, the author of man's salvation, should rightly have possessed the full vision of God from the very beginning of His Incarnation; propriety would not allow Him to have attained to it in the course of time, as other saints do. (SS 263)

Existence in God is of such a sort that it can't be added to, distinct therefore from all other existence by its very purity. . . . God in his very existing possesses all perfections. (SP 107)

Every creature is darkness in comparison with the immensity of the Divine light. (ST 1198)

This emptying of himself, by which the Invisible made Himself Visible, and the Creator and Lord of all things chose to become one of us mortal creatures, was a stooping of His mercy, not a failing of His power. (CA 2)

In Christ then was given us this wonderful deliverance, that on our passable nature the condition of death should not abide. . . . And thus through Christ is opened to us the entrance of immortal glory. (CA 2)

No one who is in a state of grace walks in darkness, according to John 8:12: *He that followeth Me, walketh not in darkness.* (ST 1206)

He alone is the Lamb without spot of sin, of whom the Father speaks, *This is my beloved Son, in whom I am well pleased.* (CA 442)

If God is mighty, it is manifest that the Son is also mighty. (CA 605)

The Son is the Offspring of the Unbegotten, One of the One, True of the True, Living of the Living, Perfect of the Perfect, Strength of Strength, Wisdom of Wisdom, Glory of Glory; the Image of the Unseen God, the Form of the Unbegotten Father. Neither can the Holy Spirit be separated from the confession of the Father and the Son. (CA 989)

He was the mediator between the Father and the world. Hence He was a doctor, by manifesting to the world the truth which He had received from the Father; He was a martyr, by suffering the persecution of the world; and He was a virgin, by His personal purity. (ST 2994)

Nothing is above the Divine Persons. (ST 1545)

From the beginning of His conception the human nature [of Christ] was united to the Divine Person, and His soul was filled with the gift of grace . . . the power of the Divine Nature, which is truly the nature of Christ, and it, moreover, belonged to Christ from the beginning of His nativity. (ST 2044)

Glory flows into the body from the soul's glory. . . . The ancient Fathers did not desire bodily strength in Christ, but spiritual strength, wherewith He vanquished the Devil and healed human weakness. (ST 2102)

In Christ each nature is united to the other in person; and by reason of this union the Divine Nature is said to be incarnate and the human nature deified. (ST 2117)

Christ came in order to bring us back from a state of bondage to a state of liberty. . . . He came in order that man might come nearer to the Divine Light, according to Luke 1:79, *To enlighten them that sit in darkness and in the shadow of death.* (ST 2210)

He worked miracles as though of His own power, and not by praying, as others do. Wherefore it is written [Lk. 6:19] that *virtue went out from Him and healed all.*

(ST 2252)

Just as the clarity which was in Christ's body was a representation of His body's future clarity, so the clarity which was in His garments signified the future clarity of the saints, which will be surpassed by that of Christ, just as the brightness of the snow is surpassed by that of the sun. (ST 2262)

Men are brought to the glory of eternal beatitude by Christ, not only those who lived after Him, but also those who preceded Him; . . . it was fitting that witnesses should be present from among those who preceded Him—namely, Moses and Elias—and from those who followed after Him—namely, Peter, James, and John. (ST 2263)

It is in Baptism that we acquire grace, while the clarity of the glory to come was foreshadowed in the transfiguration, therefore both in His Baptism and in His transfiguration the natural sonship of Christ was fittingly made known by the testimony of the Father: Because He alone with the Son and the Holy Ghost is perfectly conscious of that perfect generation. (ST 2264)

He taught that He was God; for unless this were true it would not be confirmed by miracles worked by Divine power. (ST 2252)

Christ in His human nature was not only the restorer of our nature, but was also the fountainhead of grace. . . . He knew most perfectly all that can pertain to the mysteries of grace, which transcend man's natural knowledge.

(SS 267)

He ascended into Heaven, not in His divine nature but in His human nature. In His divine nature He had never left Heaven, as He is always present everywhere. He indicates this Himself when He says: "No man hath ascended into Heaven but He that descended from Heaven, the Son of man who is in Heaven." (SS 312)

Grace is nothing else than a beginning of glory in us.

(ST 1277)

Christ by His Passion not only delivered man from sin, but also merited justifying grace for him and the glory of bliss. (ST 2267)

Much more is it God's intention to bring all things to perfection, since nature shares in this intention inasmuch as it reflects Him: hence it is written (Deut. 32:4): *The works of God are perfect.* (ST 2430)

Man's consummation consists in the attainment of his last end, which is perfect beatitude or happiness; and this consists in the vision of God. (SS 168)

Nature is not done away, but perfected by glory. (ST 1304)

The mind of man ought to be devoutly raised to the glory of eternity, which Christ restored by rising from the dead. (ST 1789)

Christ came into the world for three reasons—(1) to enlighten it ... (2) that He might reconcile it to God the Father ... (3) to deliver it from the power of the Devil. (H 80)

Things get more perfect the closer they approach some first starting point, as a thing gets brighter the nearer it gets to some supremely bright light-source. (SP 159)

The Fifth Luminous Mystery

The Institution of the Eucharist

The Eucharist

He who eats my flesh and drinks my blood has eternal life, and I will raise him up at the last day.—John 6:54

The Lord feeds His faithful ones, that they may not fail in the way of righteousness; but in their strength they may come to the table of heavenly glory. (H 98)

In the life of the body, after a man is born and becomes strong, he requires food so that his life may be preserved and sustained; so also in the life of the spirit, after being fortified, he requires spiritual food, which is Christ's body. (C 85)

We ask for our Sacramental Bread, which is prepared for us every day in the Church, praying that as we receive it sacramentally, so may it profit us unto salvation: "I am the living bread which came down from Heaven." (C 141)

In the soul of one who worthily receives this sacrament, its ... effect is to bring about the union of that man

with Christ, as He Himself says: "He that eateth my
flesh and drinketh my blood abidith in me, and I in
him." (C 263)

Aside from His many other spiritual gifts, God has made
the human soul capable of receiving the Trinity within
itself, and He nourishes it with the flesh and blood of
His beloved Son. God withheld nothing that could be
given, and this is the property of divine goodness. (W 23)

Devoutly I adore You, hidden Deity, under these appearances concealed. To You my heart surrenders self for,
seeing You, all else must yield. Sight and touch and taste
here fail; hearing only can be believed. I trust what God's
own Son has said. Truth from truth is best received. (P 69)

Allow me, I plead, to receive not only the sacrament of
Your Body and Blood but also the reality and power of
this sacrament. O most gentle God, allow me to receive
the Body of Your only-begotten Son, our Lord Jesus
Christ, Who was born of the Virgin Mary so that I might
be worthy to be united with His Mystical Body and
counted among His members. (P 75–77)

It is our duty and our privilege ever to find our gladness
in praising the most sacred Body of Christ. Is there any
employment, indeed, more congenial to Christian men
than eulogizing the abyss of divine charity? (T 24)

Wonderful, indeed, in our regard, and most worthy of
all praise, is the goodness of God, bounteous and unwea-

riedly loving, who, to meet and greet His children, in the sacrament which is the term and final realization of all sacrifices everywhere, dwells without end till the world's end. (T 25)

Lowliness, we know, is pleasing to God and it was extolled by Christ; and surely in this sacrament He preaches by example of an unrivaled lowliness, which disdains no dwelling, but consents to come as a guest to any, even a defiled, heart. (T 25)

He is whole and entire and perfect in each and every fragment of the host, as visual appearances are multiplied in a hundred mirrors. (T 26)

O unspeakable efficacy of this sacrament, which sets the affections ablaze with the fire of charity, and sprinkles our home's lintel, on either doorpost, with the blood of the immaculate Lamb! What wholesome journey-provision have we in this food for our precarious sojourning! (T 26)

It restores vigor to the weak, health to the sick; it gives increase of virtue, makes grace to abound, purges away vices, refreshes the soul, renews the life of the ailing, knits together all the faithful in the union of charity! (T 26)

This Sacrament of Faith also inspires hope and increases charity. It is the central pillar of the Church, the consolation of the dead, and the completion of Christ's Mystical Body. By these sacred species we recognize the tree of life. (T 26)

O table of the infinite God! The many marvels of this Feast amaze the mind: it is luscious beyond all dainties, delicious beyond the rarest delicacies, more fragrant than any odor, more pleasing than any form of grace, more desirable than every other food. (T 27)

O living Bread, begotten in heaven, warmed in the womb of the Virgin, baked in the furnace of the Cross, brought forth to the altar under the disguise of the wafer: strengthen my heart unto good, make it steadfast on the path through life, make glad my mind, make my thoughts pure! (T 27)

This is the true Bread which is eaten and not consumed, eaten and not dissolved, which conveys, without losing, energy. It has power to save, and it completes the work. It is the source of life and the fount of grace.

(T 27)

O chalice of sweetness which devout souls drain! O fiery cup, which sealed in Christ's blood His covenant: purge out the old leaven, make full the spirit of our minds, that we may be a new paste, feasting with the unleavened bread of sincerity and truth! (T 28)

Than His Supper can anything be more precious? . . . Christ Himself, our very God. Than this sacrament can anything be more marvelous? (T 39)

It was in order that the boundless goodness of that His great love might be driven home into the hearts of His faithful ones, that when He had celebrated the Passover with His disciples, and the last Supper was ended, . . . He loved them unto the end—and instituted this sacrament. (T 40)

This sacrament [is] the greatest miracle which He ever wrought, and the one mighty joy of them that now have sorrow, till He shall come again, and their heart shall rejoice, and their joy no man take from them. (T 40–41)

Rightly is He born in Bethlehem, which signifies the house of bread, who said, *I am the living bread, who came down from heaven.* (CA 70)

Two things may by considered in the sacrament of the Eucharist. One is the fact that it is a sacrament, and in this respect it is like the other effects of sanctifying grace. The other is that Christ's body is miraculously contained therein, and thus it is included under God's omnipotence, like all other miracles which are ascribed to God's almighty power. (ST 1177)

This sacrament works in man the effect which Christ's Passion wrought in the world. (ST 2480)

We have not a hem or a garment only of Christ, but have even His body, that we may eat thereof. If then they who touched the hem of His garment derived so much virtue therefrom, much more they that shall receive Himself whole. (CA 547)

The highest place belongs to the sacraments whereby man is sanctified: chief of which is the sacrament of the Eucharist, for it contains Christ Himself. (ST 1621–22)

The common spiritual good of the whole Church is contained substantially in the sacrament itself of the Eucharist. (ST 2378)

The water of Baptism does not cause any spiritual effect by reason of the water, but by reason of the power of the Holy Ghost, which power is in the water. . . . The true body of Christ bears the same relation to the species of bread and wine, as the power of the Holy Ghost does to the water of Baptism. (ST 2434)

Baptism is the beginning of the spiritual life, and the door of the sacraments; whereas the Eucharist is, as it were, the consummation of the spiritual life, and the end of all the sacraments. (ST 2436)

By this sacrament grace receives increase, and the spiritual life is perfected, so that man may stand perfect in himself by union with God. (ST 2480)

By Baptism a man is ordained to the Eucharist, and there-fore from the fact of children being baptized, they are destined by the Church to the Eucharist; and just as they believe through the Church's faith, so they desire the Eucharist through the Church's intention. (ST 2436)

Spiritual food changes man into itself.... As Baptism is called the sacrament of Faith, which is the founda-tion of the spiritual life, so the Eucharist is termed the sacrament of Charity, which is *the bond of perfection* (Col. 3:14). (ST 2436)

This sacrament foreshadows the Divine fruition, which shall come to pass in heaven.... And in this respect it is also called the *Eucharist*, that is, *good grace*, because *the grace of God is everlasting* (Rom. 6:23); or because it really contains Christ, Who is *full of grace*. (ST 2437)

By the blood of the Paschal Lamb the children of Israel were preserved from the destroying Angel, and brought from the Egyptian captivity; and in this respect the Paschal Lamb is the chief figure of this sacrament, because it represents it in every respect. (ST 2438)

The presence of Christ's true body and blood in this sacrament cannot be detected by sense, nor understand-ing, but by faith alone, which rests upon Divine author-ity.... Doubt not whether this be true; but take rather the Savior's words with faith. (ST 2446)

This belongs to Christ's love, out of which for our salvation He assumed a true body of our nature. And because it is the special feature of friendship to live together with friends, . . . He promises us His bodily presence as a reward. (ST 2446)

This is done by Divine power in this sacrament; for the whole substance of the bread is changed into the whole substance of Christ's body, and the whole substance of the wine into the whole substance of Christ's blood. Hence this is not a formal, but a substantial conversion. . . . It can be called *transubstantiation*. (ST 2450)

Since the Godhead never set aside the assumed body, wherever the body of Christ is, there, of necessity, must the Godhead be; and therefore it is necessary for the Godhead to be in this sacrament concomitantly with His body. (ST 2455)

This sacrament has from Christ's Passion the power of forgiving all sins, since the Passion is the fount and cause of the forgiveness of sins. (ST 2482)

The refreshment of spiritual food and the unity denoted by the species of the bread and wine are to be had in the present life, although imperfectly; but perfectly in the state of glory. . . . This sacrament does not at once admit us to glory, but bestows on us the power of coming unto glory. (ST 2481)

This sacrament preserves man from sin in both of these ways. For, first of all, by uniting man with Christ, through grace, it strengthens his spiritual life, as spiritual food and spiritual medicine. . . . Secondly, inasmuch as it is a sign of Christ's Passion, whereby the devils are conquered, it repels all the assaults of demons. (ST 2484)

The effect of the sacrament can be secured by every man if he receive it in desire, though not in reality. Consequently, just as some are baptized with the Baptism of desire, through their desire of Baptism, before being baptized in the Baptism of water; so likewise some eat this sacrament spiritually ere they receive it sacramentally. (ST 2487)

This sacrament is spiritual food; hence, just as bodily food is taken every day, so is it a good thing to receive this sacrament every day. Hence it is that our Lord (Lk. 11:3), teaches us to pray, *Give us this day our daily bread.* (ST 2498)

In this sacrament the memorial of His Passion is given by way of food which is partaken of daily; and therefore in this respect it is represented by the manna which was given daily to the people in the desert. (ST 2498)

Since the whole mystery of our salvation is comprised in this sacrament, therefore is it performed with greater solemnity than the other sacraments. (ST 2517)

The infusion of grace removes venial sins. . . . And so, by the Eucharist, Extreme Unction, and by all the sacraments of the New Law without exception, wherein grace is conferred, venial sins are remitted.   (ST 2552)

It is manifest that the sacraments of the Church derive their power specially from Christ's Passion. . . . It was in sign of this that from the side of Christ hanging on the Cross there flowed water and blood, the former of which belongs to Baptism, the latter to the Eucharist, which are the principal sacraments.   (ST 2359)

OTHER TOPICS

Prayer

Watch and pray that you may not enter into temptation.
— Mark 14:38

The just cry manifoldly—firstly, in praying; secondly, in confessing; thirdly, in praising. (H 16)

The Word of God abiding in us should be continually in our thoughts, since not only should we believe in Him, but also meditate upon Him; otherwise we would derive no profit from His presence. In fact, meditation of this kind is of great assistance against sin. (C 27)

Among all prayers the Lord's Prayer stands preeminent, for it excels in the five conditions required in prayer: confidence, rectitude, order, devotion, and humility.
(C 103)

Prayer should be confident: "Let us go with confidence to the throne of grace" (Heb. 4:16) and with fullness of faith: "Let him ask in faith, nothing wavering." (C 103)

There can be no doubt that the Lord's Prayer affords the greatest security, since it was framed by our Advocate and most wise Petitioner, in whom are "all the treasures of wisdom." (C 103)

Prayer should be humble: "He hath had regard to the prayer of the humble." This is seen in the story of the Pharisee and the publican, and is expressed in the words of Judith: "The prayer of the humble and the meek hath always pleased Thee." (C 105–6)

As desire should be orderly, so should prayer, since it is the expression of desire. Now, the right order is that our desires and prayers should prefer spiritual goods to carnal goods and heavenly things to earthly things: "Seek ye first the kingdom of God and His justice, and all these things shall be added unto you." (Matt. 6:33) (C 105)

Devotion arises from charity, which is the love of God and of our neighbor, and both of these are indicated in the Lord's Prayer. In order to express of love of God we call Him *Father*, and in order to indicate our love of neighbor we pray for all in general. (C 105)

If our prayer is not granted, it is either because it lacks constancy, in that "we should pray always and never faint," or because we ask for what is less conductive to our salvation. (C 107)

If you say the words with your lips, fulfill them in your heart. (C 147)

Just as the tired body desires rest, so also does the soul. But the soul's proper rest is in God: "Be Thou unto me a God, a protector, and a house of refuge." (C 197)

They [the heavenly bodies] serve man in the sense that by their beauty and enormous size they show forth the excellence of their Creator. For this reason man is often exhorted in Sacred Scripture to contemplate the heavenly bodies, so as to be moved by them to sentiments of reverence toward God. (SS 191)

We do not pray to change divine decree, but only to obtain what God has decided will be obtained through prayer. In other words, as St. Gregory says, "by asking, men deserve to receive what the all-powerful God has decreed from all eternity to give them." (P intro)

Prayer, then, for obtaining something from God, is necessary for man on account of the very one who prays, that he many reflect on his shortcomings and may turn his mind to desiring fervently and piously what he hopes to gain by his petition. In this way he is rendered fit to receive the favor. (SS 335)

When we pray to God, the very prayer we send forth makes us intimate with Him, inasmuch as our soul is raised up to God, converses with Him in spiritual affection, and adores Him in spirit and truth. (SS 335)

In prayer to God, perseverance or repetition of our supplication is not unseemly, but is acceptable to God. Indeed, "we ought always to pray and not to faint," as we learn from Luke 18:1. Our Lord, too, invites us to pray, for He said: "Ask, and it shall be given you.... Knock, and it shall be opened to you." (SS 336)

He would not urge us to pray unless He were determined to hear us. (SS 337)

If he hopes to receive . . . a benefit from a man, his request is called *simple petition*; if he hopes to obtain a favor from God, it is called *prayer*. (SS 346–47)

Truth is the end of contemplation. (T 194)

Through loving God we are aflame to gaze on His beauty. And since every one rejoices when he obtains what he loves, it follows that the contemplative life terminates in delight . . . the result being that love also becomes more intense. (T 194)

The most perfect bliss consists in contemplation. Having perfection that also overflows into others is more perfect than just having it oneself. (SP 323)

We have power before God by the sweet savor of our prayers. (CA 77)

Solomon says, *Before prayer, prepare thy soul.* . . . Good works stir up the faith of the heart, and give the soul confidence in prayer to God. Alms then are a preparation for prayer, and therefore the Lord after speaking of alms proceeds accordingly to instruct us concerning prayer. (CA 217)

The mental posture of prayer calms and purifies the soul, and makes it of more capacity to receive the divine gifts which are poured into it. For God does not hear us for the prevailing force of our pleadings; He is at all times ready to give us His light, but we are not ready to receive it, but prone to other things. (CA 222)

We say not My Father, but *Our Father*, for the teacher of peace and master of unity would not have men pray singly and severally, since when any prays, he is not to pray for himself only. (CA 223–24)

We daily make petition, since we need a daily sanctification, in order that we who sin day by day, may cleanse afresh our offenses by a continual sanctification. (CA 225)

Knock, and it shall be opened to you. . . . Knock with prayer, and fasting, and alms. For as one who knocks at a door, not only cries out with his voice, but strikes with his hand, so he who does good works, knocks with his works. (CA 272)

As physicians are gained by money, so [is God] with prayer. We offer to God nothing more worthy than faithful prayer. (CA 299)

Solitude is good, when we have need to pray to God. For this also He goes into the desert, and there spends the night in prayer, to teach us that for prayer we should seek stillness both in time and place. (CA 539)

There is nothing more powerful than a man who prays properly. (CA 615)

He shows His devotion in His prayer, and as beloved and well-pleasing to His Father, He adds, *Not as I will, but as thou wilt*, teaching us that we should pray, not that our own will, but that God's will, should be done. (CA 909)

Although one is not bound to pray at all hours, one is bound throughout the day to keep oneself fit for prayer. (ST 2805)

Man's most perfect thoughts are those which are about God.... He is the fount of all goodness: and thus it is altogether impossible to think of Him without delight. (ST 3006)

Through meditation man conceives the thought of surrendering himself to God's service.... He needs to lean on God. (ST 1536)

When we pray we ought principally to ask to be united to God, according to Psalm 26:4, *One thing I have asked of the Lord, this will I seek after, that I may dwell in the house of the Lord all the days of my life*. (ST 1538)

We need to pray to God, not in order to make known to Him our needs or desires, but that we ourselves may be reminded of the necessity of having recourse to God's help in these matters. (ST 1539)

When in our prayers we ask for things concerning our salvation, we conform our will to God's, of Whom it is written (1 Tim. 2:4) that *He will have all men to be saved.* (ST 1541)

We ought to pray even for sinners, that they may be converted, and for the just that they persevere and advance in holiness. . . . No man should be denied the help of prayer. (ST 1542–43)

The Lord's Prayer is most perfect. . . . Now in the Lord's Prayer not only do we ask for all that we may rightly desire, but also in the order wherein we ought to desire them, so that this prayer not only teaches us to ask, but also directs all our affections. (ST 1544)

Vocal prayer is employed, not in order to tell God something He does not know, but in order to lift up the mind of the person praying or of other persons to God. . . . Words signifying some object of devotion lift up the mind, especially one that is less devout. (ST 1547)

Even holy men sometimes suffer from a wandering of the mind when they pray. . . . It is not necessary that prayer should be attentive throughout; because the force of the original intention with which one sets about praying renders the whole prayer meritorious, as is the case with other meritorious acts. (ST 1548)

The very act of praying is *a gift of God*, as Augustine states. (ST 1550)

There are three kinds of attention that can be brought to vocal prayer: one which attends to the words, lest we say them wrong, another which attends to the sense of the words, and a third, which attends to the end of prayer, namely, God, and to the things we are praying for. That last kind of attention is most necessary. (ST 1548)

Faith is necessary in reference to God to Whom we pray; that is, we need to believe that we can obtain from Him what we seek. Humility is necessary on the part of the person praying, because he recognizes his neediness.
(ST 1550)

Ask—*for ourselves*—*things necessary for salvation*—*piously*—*perseveringly*; when all these four concur, we always obtain what we ask for. (ST 1550)

Prayer is the *raising up of one's mind to God*. (ST 1551)

External actions are signs of internal reverence. (ST 1553)

We offer to God a twofold adoration; namely, a spiritual adoration, consisting in the internal devotion of the mind; and a bodily adoration, which consists in an exterior humbling of the body. (ST 1553)

The goods of the soul, such as contemplation and prayer, far surpass the goods of the body and still more conform us to God. (ST 1576)

Prayer is primarily in the mind, and secondarily expressed in words. . . . So too adoration consists chiefly in an interior reverence of God, but secondarily in certain bodily signs of humility; thus when we genuflect we signify our weakness in comparison with God, and when we prostrate ourselves we profess that we are nothing of ourselves. (ST 1553)

We need to praise God with our lips, not indeed for His sake, but for our own sake; since by praising Him our devotion is aroused towards Him. . . . Forasmuch as man, by praising God, ascends in his affections to God, by so much is he withdrawn from things opposed to God. (ST 1589)

It profits one nothing to praise with the lips if one praise not with the heart. For the heart speaks God's praises when it fervently recalls *the glorious things of His works.* Yet the outward praise of the lips avails to arouse the inward fervor of those who praise, and to incite others to praise God. (ST 1590)

There is in man a natural inclination to set aside a certain time for each necessary thing, such as refreshment of the body, sleep, and so forth. Hence according to the dictate of reason, man sets aside a certain time for spiritual refreshment, by which man's mind is refreshed in God. (ST 1701)

Idleness is removed by meditation on the Holy Scriptures and by the divine praises. (ST 1986)

Among the works of the contemplative life prayer is greater than study. (ST 1999)

Christ wished to pray to His Father in order to give us an example of praying; and also to show that His Father is the author both of His eternal procession in the Divine Nature, and of all the good that He possesses in the human nature. (ST 2140)

When it is said that in raising Lazarus He lifted up His eyes (Jn. 11:41), this was not because He needed to pray, but because He wished to teach us how to pray. (ST 2251)

The prayers of a multitude are more easily heard. (ST 1543)

Common prayer is that which is offered to God by the ministers of the Church representing the body of the faithful: it is reasonably ordained that the ministers of the Church should say these prayers even in a loud voice, so that they may come to the knowledge of all. (ST 1547)

Feast days were instituted for that spiritual joy which is the effect of prayer. Therefore, on such days our prayers should be multiplied. (C 195)

Our motive in praying is, not that we may change the Divine disposition, but that, by our prayers, we may obtain what God has appointed. (ST 1539)

The Essence of God

I tell you most solemnly, before Abraham was, I am.
—John 8:58

Only when acted on by a first cause do intermediate causes produce a change; unless a hand moves the stick, the stick won't move anything else. So we are forced eventually to come to a first cause of change not itself being changed by anything, and this is what everyone understands by God. (SP 200)

Some things are found to be better, truer, more excellent than others. . . . So there is something that causes in all other things their being, their goodness, and whatever other perfections they have. And this is what we call *God*. (SP 201)

God's existing is individually distinguished from all other existing by the very fact that it is an existing subsistent in itself, and not one supervening on a nature other than existing itself. (SP 207)

Eternity is called whole not because it has parts but because it has nothing lacking to it. (SP 211)

Eternity is simultaneously whole, while in time there is before and after. So time and eternity differ. . . . The infinite is immeasurable. (SP 212–13)

God is alive doesn't mean life pours out from him, but expresses the fact that life pre-exists in him as the source of all things, though in a way surpassing anything we can understand or express. (SP 219)

His goodness is his substance, and his wisdom is his substance, and so on. These words are completely synonymous. (SP 221)

The very fact that God contains in one simple unity what other things share in many different ways shows the perfection of God's unity. (SP 222–23)

God is called omniscient in the same way as he's called omnipotent. But he's called omniscient because he knows absolutely everything; so he must be called omnipotent because he can do absolutely everything. (SP 247)

As long as creatures exist this comes from God, just as long as the air is lit up this comes from the sun. (SP 262)

If you want to know why the heavens are so big and not bigger, the only answer is that he who made it wanted it that size. . . . Scripture urges us to look at the stars, since their order above all shows how everything is subject to the will and providence of the creator. (SP 266)

God's action is eternal, since it is his very substance. (SP 269)

God does precede the world in duration, but in eternity, not in time, since God's existence is not measured by time. There was no real time before the world existed. . . . While eternity existed, unlimited periods of time could have rolled by. (SP 270)

Just as God's existence embraces in its power everything else that exists in any way whatever, thus sharing in a sense in God's existence, so too God's understanding and what he understands embraces all knowledge and all things that can be known, and God's will and what he wills embraces all desiring and all good things that can be desired. (SP 281)

God's knowing . . . is altogether outside time, as if he stands on the summit of eternity where everything exists together, looking down in a single simple glance on the whole course of time. (SP 282)

God's power is at work in nature's own activity in the way a principal agent's power is at work in the activity of a tool. . . . God and nature are hierarchically related.

(SP 304)

We should hope from Him nothing less than Himself, since His goodness, whereby he imparts good things to His creature, is no less than His Essence. Therefore the proper and principal object of hope is eternal happiness.

(ST 1243)

The very name of the Godhead implies a kind of watching over things. . . . God's omnipotence includes, in a way, universal knowledge and providence. For He would not be able to do all He wills in things here below, unless He knew them, and exercised His providence over them. (ST 1176)

The more perfectly do we know God in this life, the more we understand that He surpasses all that the mind comprehends. (ST 1209)

God is as lovable as He is good, and His goodness is infinite, wherefore He is infinitely lovable. (ST 1281)

Nature gives glory to her Framer. (CA 284)

All things are less than God's power. (CA 294)

The object of the Divine love which is God surpasses the judgment of reason, wherefore it is not measured by reason but transcends it. (ST 1309)

It belongs to mercy to be bountiful to others, and, what is more, to succor others in their wants, which pertain chiefly to one who stands above. Hence mercy is accounted as being proper to God: and therein His omnipotence is declared to be chiefly manifested. (ST 1320)

He alone has immortality, and is the fount of life, wherefore He is rightly called God the Father; for He is life as it were flowing out of a fountain, who said, *I am the life*. (CA 582)

Some of His effects are such that they nowise be contrary to the human will, *since to be, to live, to understand*, which are effects of God, are desirable and lovable to all. God draws all things to Himself. (ST 1341)

Who is He but God, who created all men, who being by nature Lord of all, yet would rather be loved as a father, than feared as a Lord. (CA 724)

It belongs to human nature to come and go. Divine nature remains ever the same. (CA 889)

There are things which the blessed, whether angels or men, do not know: such things are not essential to blessedness, but concern the government of things according to Divine Providence. (ST 1414)

God's will alone is perpetual. (ST 1435)

Man sees not the heart as God does. (ST 2798)

Matters concerning the Godhead are, in themselves, the strongest incentive to love and consequently to devotion, because God is supremely lovable. (ST 1536)

It is clear that the essence of bliss consists in seeing God. Therefore the Godhead cannot be seen without joy. Further, the essence of the Godhead is the essence of truth. Now it is delightful to everyone to see the truth, wherefore *all naturally desire to know.* (ST 2948)

The renewal of the world is directed to the end that, after this renewal has taken place, God may become visible to man by signs so manifest as to be perceived as it were by his senses. Now creatures lead to the knowledge of God chiefly by their comeliness and beauty, which show forth the wisdom of their Maker and Governor.

(ST 2954)

Whatever form our intellect conceive, that form is out of proportion to the Divine essence. Hence He cannot be fathomed by our intellect: but our most perfect knowledge of Him as wayfarers is to know that He is above all that our intellect can conceive. . . . In heaven, however, we shall see Him by a form which is His essence, and we shall be united to Him. (ST 2962)

Honor is due to someone under the aspect of excellence: and to God a singular excellence is competent, since He infinitely surpasses all things and exceeds them in every way. (ST 1531)

The vision of God cannot be without delight. (ST 1916)

Nothing is wanting to the perfection of the Divine Nature. (ST 2047)

It would seem most fitting that by visible things the invisible things of God should be made known; for to this end was the whole world made. . . . By the mystery of the Incarnation are made known at once the goodness, the wisdom, the justice, and the power or might of God.

(ST 2025–26)

The Word of God is the principle of all life. (ST 2038)

God Himself is happy and rich in Himself—that is, in the enjoyment of Himself. Now a man's inheritance is that which makes him rich. Wherefore, inasmuch as God, of His goodness, admits men to the inheritance of beatitude, He is said to adopt them. (ST 2147)

Man works in order to supply his wants: not so God, Who works in order to communicate to others the abundance of His perfection. (ST 2147)

All places put together could not comprise His immensity; rather is it His immensity that embraces all things. . . . If a whole be in some place, then no part of it is outside that place. But this is not the case with God. (ST 2304)

God exists always. . . . Nothing brings itself forth from potency to act or from non-being to being. But God can have no cause of His being, since He is the first Being; a cause is prior to what is caused. Of necessity, therefore, God must always have existed. (SS 12–13)

Whatever is caused is finite, since only God's essence is infinite. (SS 67)

God's essence is His existence. This sublime truth Moses was taught by the Lord: for when he asked the Lord: *If the children of Israel should say to me: What is His name? what shall I say to them?* the Lord answered: *I AM WHO AM. . . . Thus shalt thou say to the children of Israel: HE WHO IS hath sent me to you;* thus declaring His own name to be *HE WHO IS.* (T 124)

Nothing is so like God as the human soul. And the manner of generation in the soul is that a man by his soul conceives something which is called the concept of the mind. This concept proceeds from the soul as from its father, and is called the word of the mind or of man. . . . Thus the Son of God is nothing else but the Word of God. (C 26)

Even the unlearned perceive how ridiculous it is to suppose that instruments are moved, unless they are set in motion by some principal agent. This would be like fancying that, when a chest or a bed is being built, the saw or the hatchet performs its functions without a carpenter. Accordingly, there must be a first mover that is above all the rest; and this being we call God. (SS 9)

He possesses infinite power, from which nothing can be taken away. And this includes the further truth that He is infinite and perfect; for the power of a thing follows the perfections of its essence. (SS 33–34)

The child is not begotten except by a man and the seed does not receive existence except from an animal or a plant. Accordingly, that which is by nature prior to all other things and sets them in motion, must be more perfect than all the rest. (SS 23)

The builder requires stones and lumber before he can set to work, because he is unable to produce these materials by his action. On the other hand, he does not presuppose a house, but produces it by his activity. But matter must be produced by God's action since everything that exists in any way at all has God as the cause of its existence. (SS 64)

A man who is free to walk or not to walk, walks when he wills. Hence effects proceed from God according to the determination of His will. And so He acts, not by a necessity of His nature, but by His will. This is why the Catholic Faith calls the omnipotent God not only *Creator*, but also *Maker*. For making is properly the action of an artificer who operates by his will. (SS 101)

The very order existing among diverse things issues in a certain beauty, which should call to mind the divine wisdom. (SS 112–13)

God is necessarily present to all things to the extent that they have existence. But existence is that which is the most intimately present in all things. Therefore God must be in all things. (SS 147)

God knows, in His eternity, all that takes place throughout the whole course of time. For His eternity is in
present contact with the whole course of time, and even
passes beyond time. We may fancy that God knows the
flight of time in His eternity, in the way that a person
standing on top of a watchtower embraces in a single
glance a whole caravan of passing travelers. (SS 150–51)

We sufficiently express our conviction that the divine
will is ready to help us when we proclaim that God is
our Father. But to exclude all doubt as to the perfection
of His power, we add: "who art in Heaven." The Father
is not said to be in Heaven as though He were contained
by Heaven. On the contrary, He encompasses Heaven
in His power. (SS 342–43)

God is the first cause. Therefore He did not begin to
be. Therefore neither will He cease to be: because that
which always was, has the power to be always. Therefore He is eternal. (T 99)

The power of the first mover is an infinite power. (T 109)

We are able to gather the wisdom of God from the
consideration of His works, since by a kind of communication of His likeness it is spread abroad in the things
He has made. (T 174)

When Moses sought to see the face of God, the Lord
answered him: *I will show thee all good,* giving thus to
understand that the fullness of all good is in Him. (T 141)

We do not, therefore, know God by seeing His essence, but from the pattern of the whole universe. . . . For the ordered universe has some likeness and faint resemblance to the divine nature which is its pattern and archetype. Thus from consideration of the ordered universe, *we ascend in ordered degrees, so far as we are able from our intellect*, to God Who is above all. (T 188)

The divine wisdom is the efficient cause wherefrom all things receive their being, and not their being only, but also their order in the cosmos, in so far as things conspire together and collaborate to one last end. Wisdom fashions the beauty of the universe, *producing one beautiful harmony and agreement of all things*, in due order and proportion. (T 190–91)

As the movement flowing from the soul to the body is the life of the body, so the movement whereby the universe is moved by God is, so to speak, a certain life of the universe. (SS 166)

THE CHURCH

So now I say to you: You are Peter and on this rock I will build my Church. And the gates of the underworld can never hold out against it. —Matthew 16:18

Just as one man has one soul and one body yet many members, so the Catholic Church is one body, having many members. The soul that gives life to this body is the Holy Spirit. So after confessing our belief in the Holy Spirit, we are bid to believe in the Holy Catholic Church. (C 77)

The Holy Church signifies the assembly of the faithful, and the individual Christian is a member of the Church of which it is said: "Draw near to me, ye unlearned, and gather yourselves together into the house of discipline." (C 77)

Wherever God dwells, that place is holy.... "Holiness becometh Thy house, O Lord." (C 79–80)

The Church of Peter flourishes in faith and is immune from error. Nor need we wonder at this, since the Lord said to Peter, "I have prayed for thee, Peter, that thy faith may not fail." (C 82)

The Church's chief foundation is Christ. . . . The Apostles and their doctrine are the Church's secondary foundation, from which she derives her stability. This is described where it is said that the city had "twelve foundations, wherein were (inscribed) the names of the twelve Apostles." Hence the Church is called *apostolic*. (C 81)

A house also is proved to be firmly built if, however much it is shaken, it remains standing. And the Church has ever proved indestructible. Her persecutors have failed to destroy her. In fact, it was during times of persecution that the Church grew more and more. (C 81)

Nor has the Church failed before the assaults of demons, for she is like a tower of refuge to all who fight against the devil. . . . Hence the devil does his utmost to destroy the Church, but he does not prevail, for our Lord said that "the gates of hell shall not prevail against it." (C 82)

There are seven sacraments of the New Law. . . . The first five of these sacraments are intended to bring about the perfection of the individual man in himself; the other two sacraments—Holy Orders and Matrimony—are so constituted that they perfect and multiply the entire Church. (C 254)

We are all embarked in the vessel of the Holy Church, and voyaging through this stormy world with the Lord. (CA 323)

When the Lord founded His Church, it was not nobles and men of great learning, but simple fishermen whom He established as princes over the whole earth, confiding to them the government of the Church. As the Apostle said: "But the foolish things of the world hath God chosen, in order that He may confound the wise." (W 51)

From the fact that the singular grace of Christ's soul is infinite . . . we readily infer that the grace which is His as head of the Church is also infinite. For the very reason that He possesses it, He pours it forth. (SS 261)

The army of the Church is higher in status than the army of the world; its warfare is a higher one, and its soldiers fight against spiritual enemies. . . . *For the weapons of our warfare are not carnal*, but spiritual, set by God unto the destruction of error, vice, and sin. (T 8)

For the Church the more zealously she removes from the earthly to the heavenly, the more she abounds in the flower and fruit of virtues. (CA 89)

The universal Church cannot err, since she is governed by the Holy Ghost, Who is the Spirit of Truth: for such was Our Lord's promise to His disciples [Jn. 16:13]: *When He, the Spirit of truth, is come, He will teach you all truth.* (ST 1177)

The ministers of the Church have no power to publish new articles of faith, or to do away with those which are already published, or to institute new sacraments, or to abolish those that are instituted, for this belongs to the power of excellence, which belongs to Christ alone, Who is the foundation of the Church. (ST 2591)

The spiritual fruit of the Church is derived not only from her prayers, but also from the sacraments received and from the faithful dwelling together. (ST 2641)

The Church Militant is the way to the Church Triumphant. (ST 2644)

Since the baptismal character whereby a man is numbered among God's people, is indelible, one who is baptized always belongs to the Church in some way. (ST 2646)

The saints in whom this super-abundance of satisfactions is found, did not perform their good works for this or that particular person, who needs the remission of his punishment. . . . But they performed them for the whole Church in general, even as the Apostle declares that he fills up *those things that are wanting of the sufferings of Christ*. (ST 2652)

Our Lord said to His disciples [Lk. 10:16]: *He that hears you heareth Me*. Therefore a commandment of the Church has the same force as a commandment of God. (ST 2760)

Christ is fittingly called the Head of the Church. . . . The head has a manifest pre-eminence over the other exterior members; but the heart has a certain hidden influence. And hence the Holy Ghost is likened to the heart, since He invisibly quickens and unifies the Church. (ST 2076)

In order the more to show His power, He set up the head of His Church in Rome itself, which was the head of the world, in sign of His complete victory, in order that from that city the faith might spread throughout the world. (ST 2209)

Christ is established by God the Head of the Church— yea, of all men, . . . so that not only all men might receive grace through Him, but that all might receive the doctrine of Truth from Him. (ST 2096)

The Apostles, led by the inward instinct of the Holy Ghost, handed down to the churches certain instructions which they did not put in writing, but which have been ordained, in accordance with the observance of the Church as practiced by the faithful as time went on. Wherefore the Apostle says [2 Thess. 2:14]: *Stand fast; and hold the traditions which you have learned, whether by word*, that is by word of mouth—*or by our epistle*—that is by word put into writing. (ST 2156)

The Church does nothing in vain. (ST 2422)

The bishop receives power to act on Christ's behalf upon His mystical body, that is, upon the Church. . . . It belongs to the bishop to deliver, not only to the people, but likewise to priests, such things as serve them in the fulfillment of their respective duties. (ST 2504)

The Church's ordinances are Christ's own ordinances. (ST 2515)

Christ's holiness is the fount of all the Church's holiness. (ST 2515)

He who adheres to the teaching of the Church, as to an infallible rule, assents to whatever the Church teaches. (ST 1199)